RECORDED VERSIONS GUITAR

**AUTHENTIC TRANSCRIPTIONS
WITH NOTES AND TABLATURE**

MW01195252

BULLET FOR MY VALENTINE
SCREAM AIM FIRE

WWW.BULLETFORMYVALENTINE1.COM
WWW.MYSPACE.COM/BULLETFORMYVALENTINE

Arranged by Olly Weeks
Edited by Lucy Holliday & Alex Davis

Managed by Craig Jennings for Raw Power Management
www.rawpowermanagement.com
Assisted by Tristan Lillingston

Art Direction + Design: Jeff Gilligan
Photo-illustrations by Don Clark for Invisible Creature
Photography: Chapman Baehler

Printed in England by Caligraving Ltd
All rights reserved

The text paper used in this publication is a virgin fibre product that is manufactured in the UK to ISO 14001 standards.
The wood fibre used is only sourced from managed forests using sustainable forestry principles.
This paper is 100% recyclable.

HAL•LEONARD® CORPORATION

7777 W. BLUEMOUND RD. P.O. BOX 13819 MILWAUKEE, WI 53213

ISBN 978-1-4234-5819-7

In Australia Contact:
Hal Leonard Australia Pty. Ltd.
4 Lentara Court
Cheltenham, Victoria, 3192, Australia
Email: ausadmin@halleonard.com.au

Visit Hal Leonard Online at
www.halleonard.com

BULLET FOR MY VALENTINE
SCREAM AIM FIRE

SCREAM AIM FIRE

Words and Music by Matthew Tuck, Jason James,
Michael Paget and Michael Thomas

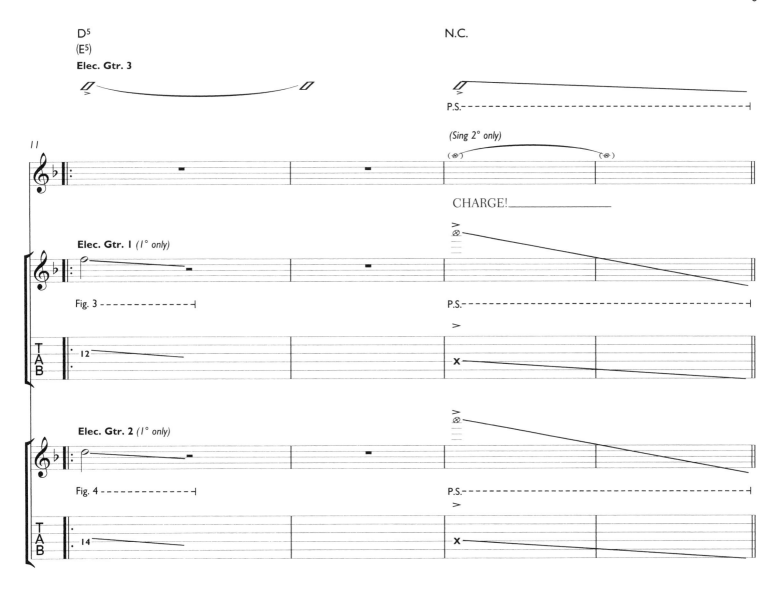

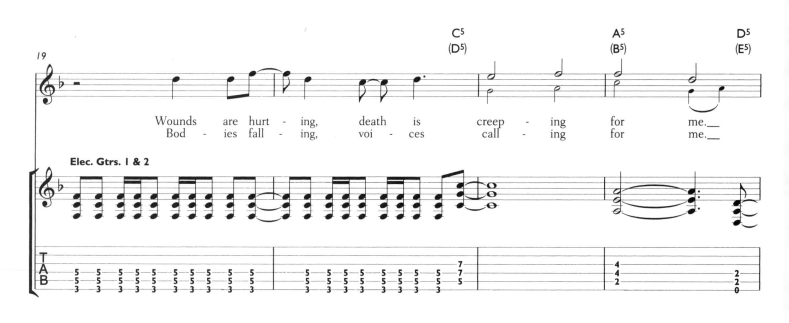

Wounds are hurt - ing, death is creep - ing for me.___
Bod - ies fall - ing, voi - ces call - ing for me.___

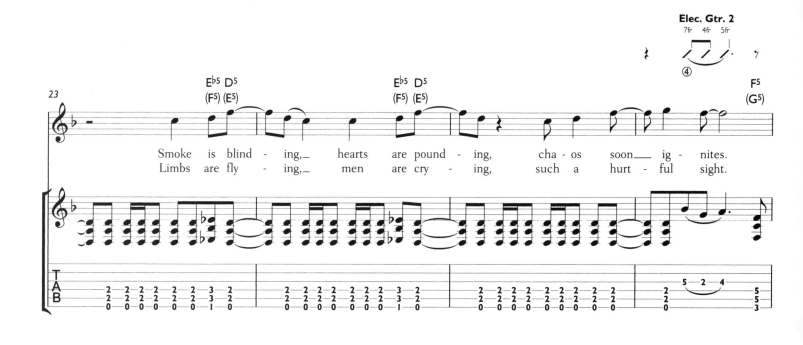

Smoke is blind - ing,___ hearts are pound - ing, cha - os soon___ ig - nites.
Limbs are fly - ing,___ men are cry - ing, such a hurt - ful sight.

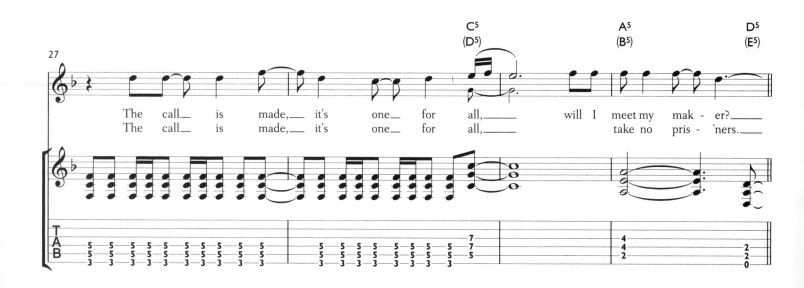

The call___ is made,___ it's one___ for all,_____ will I meet my mak - er?_____
The call___ is made,___ it's one___ for all,_____ take no pris - 'ners.___

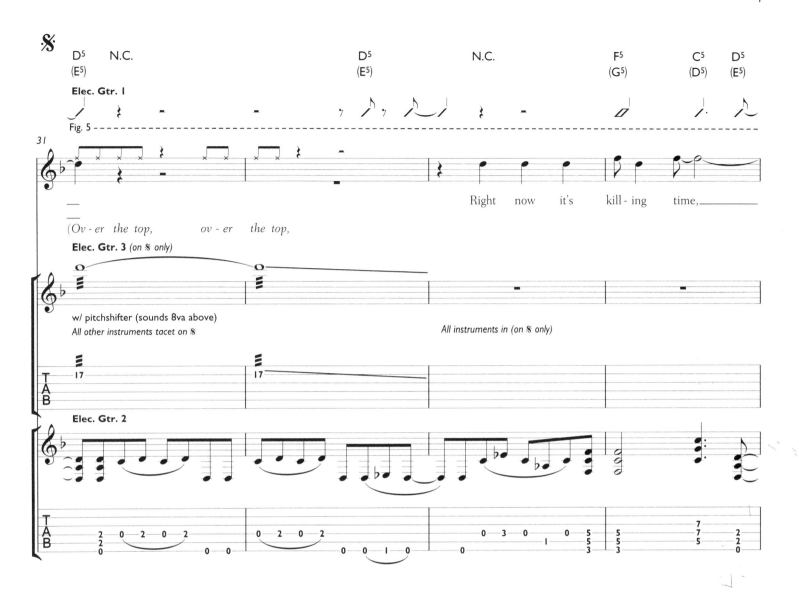

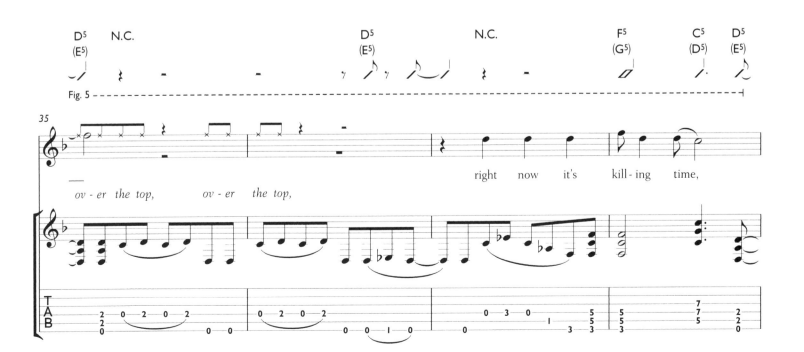

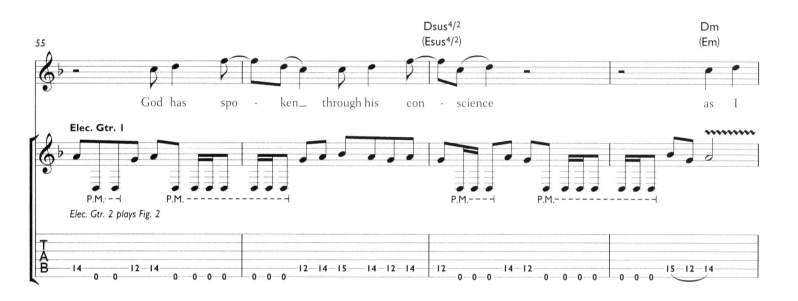

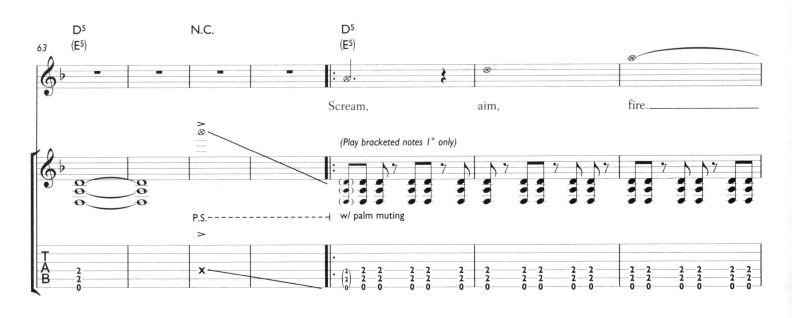

Scream,   aim,   fire.

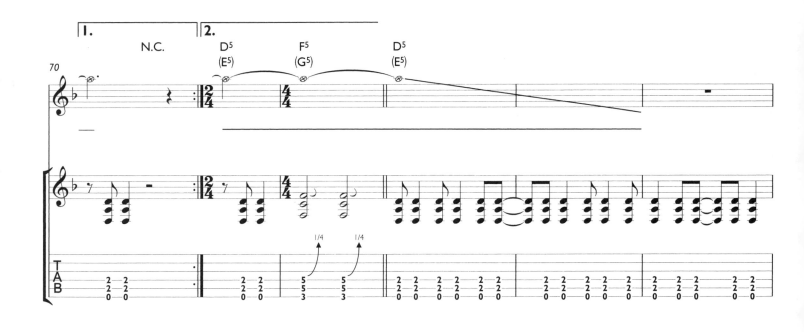

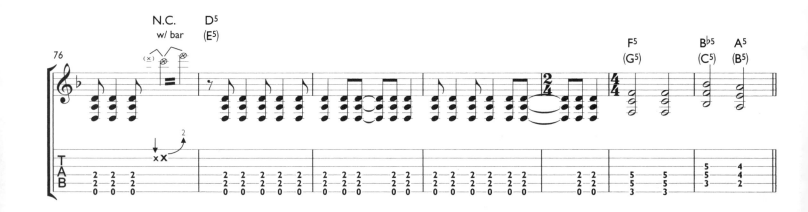

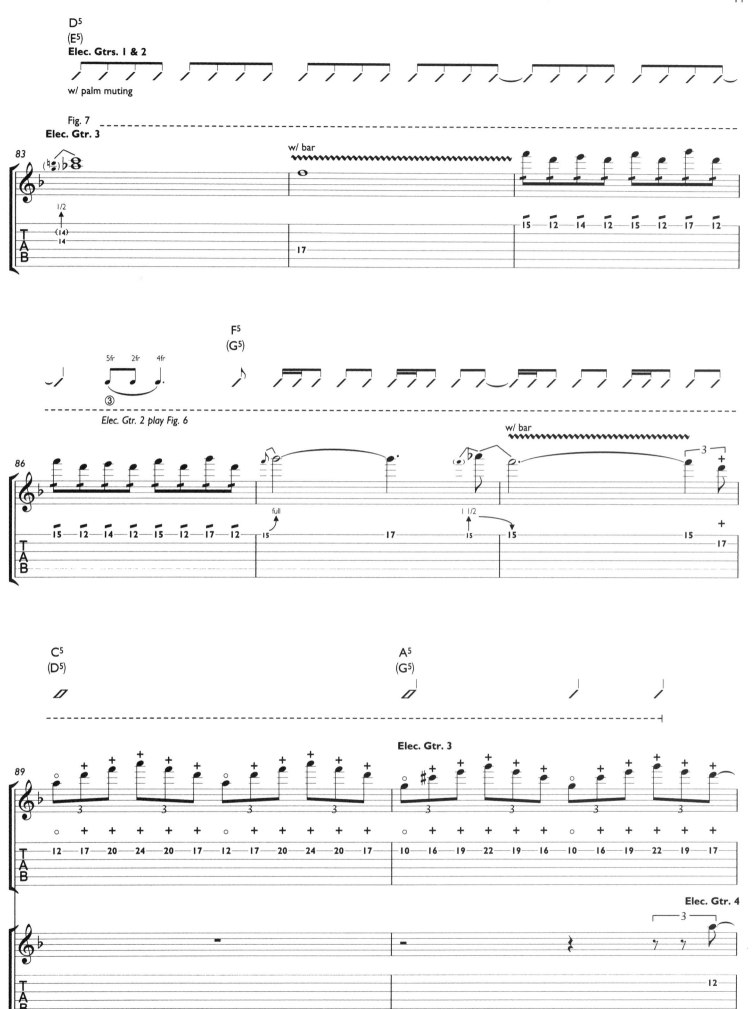

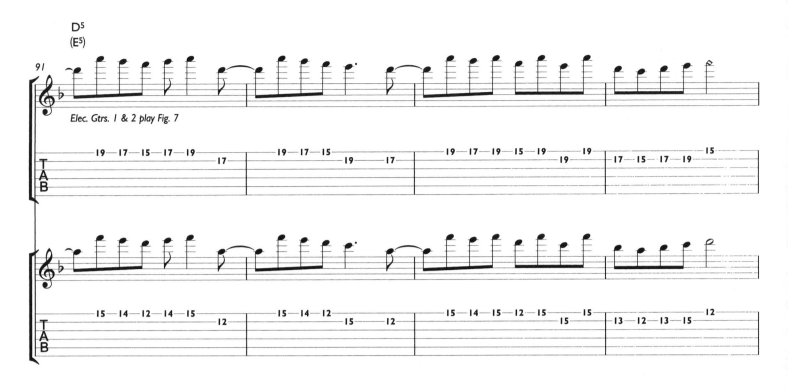

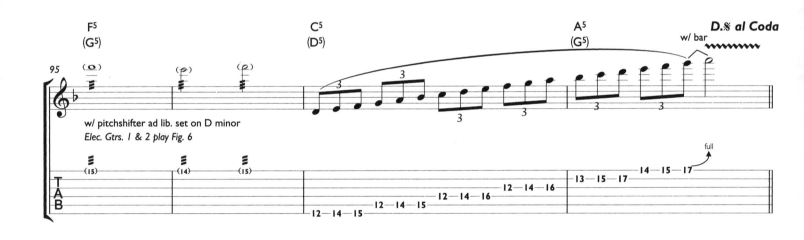

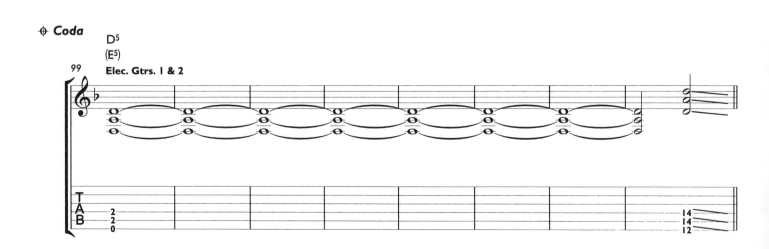

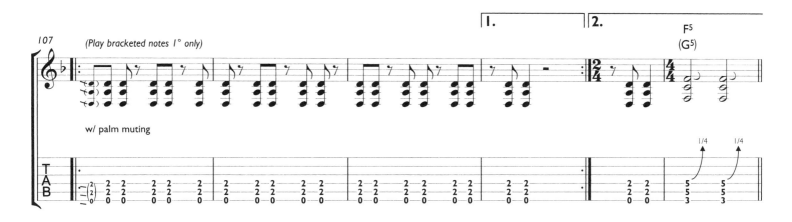

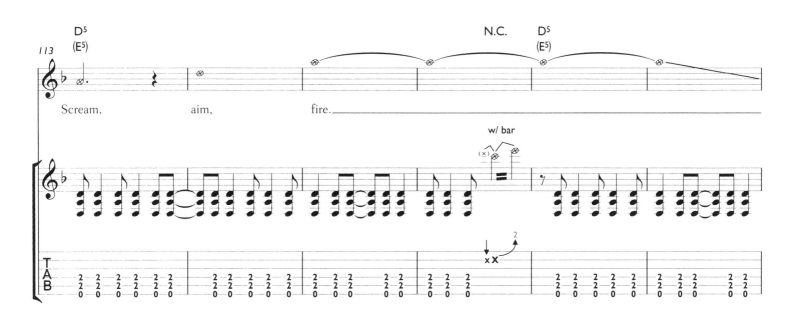

Scream, aim, fire.

EYE OF THE STORM

Words and Music by Matthew Tuck, Jason James,
Michael Paget and Michael Thomas

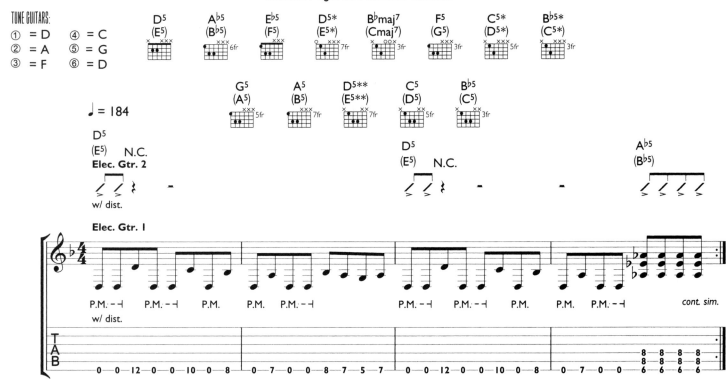

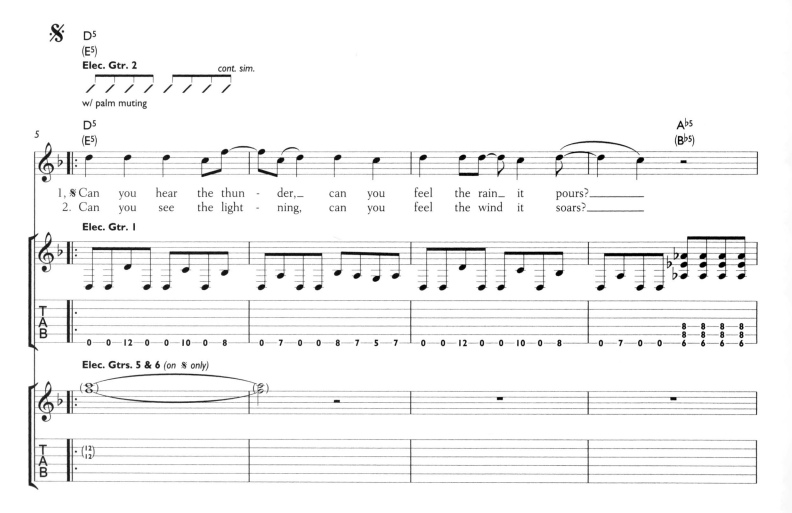

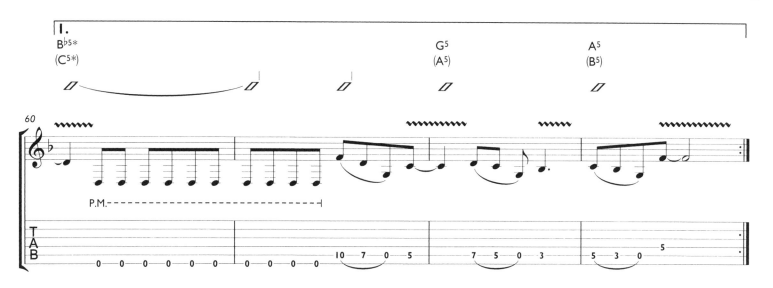

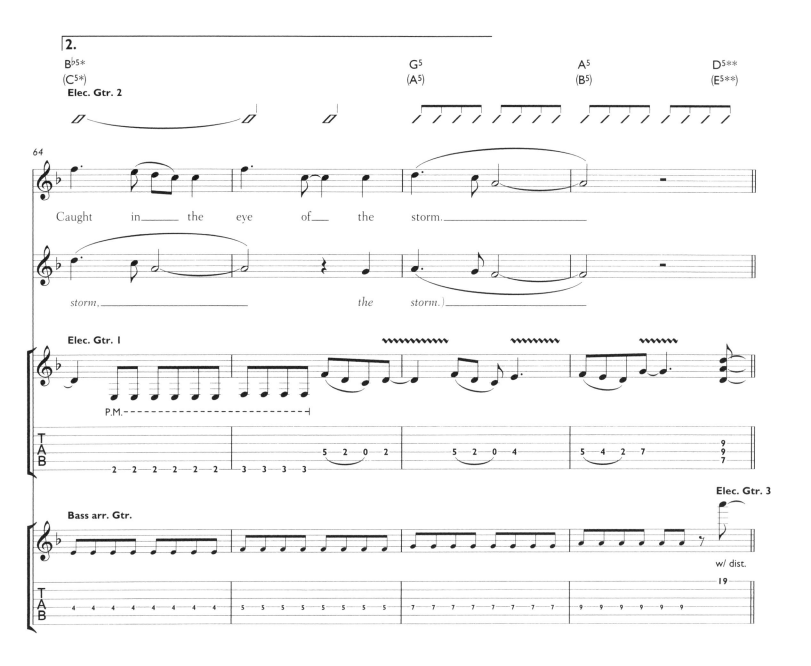

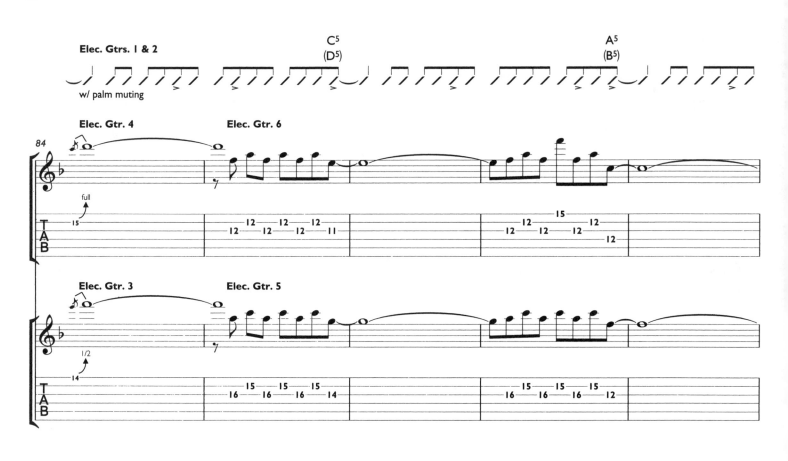

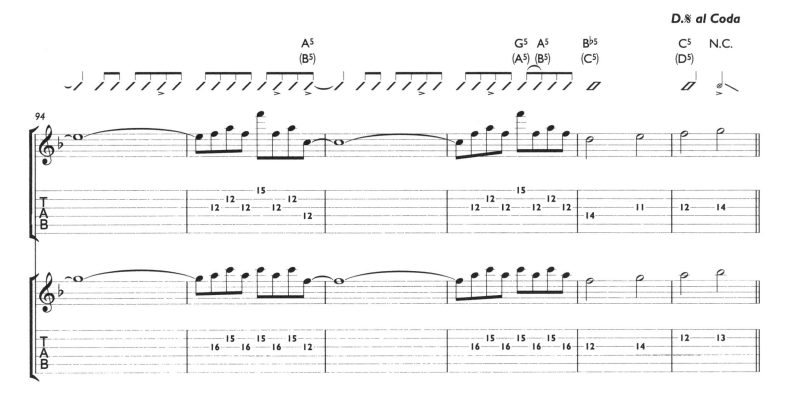

HEARTS BURST INTO FIRE

Words and Music by Matthew Tuck, Jason James,
Michael Paget and Michael Thomas

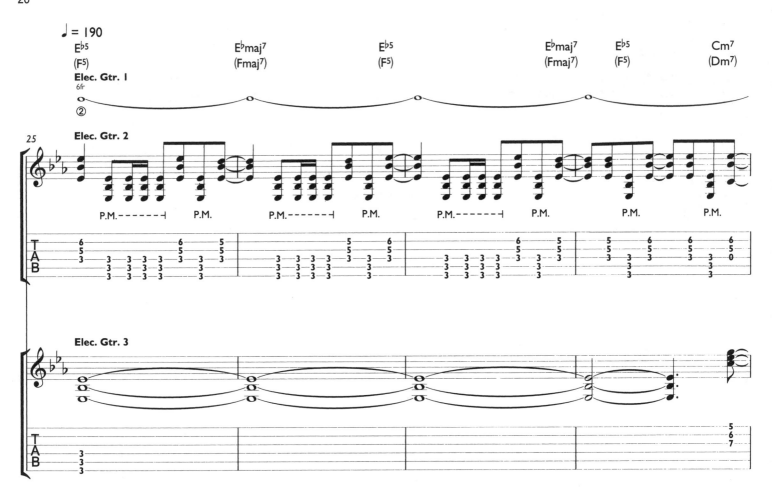

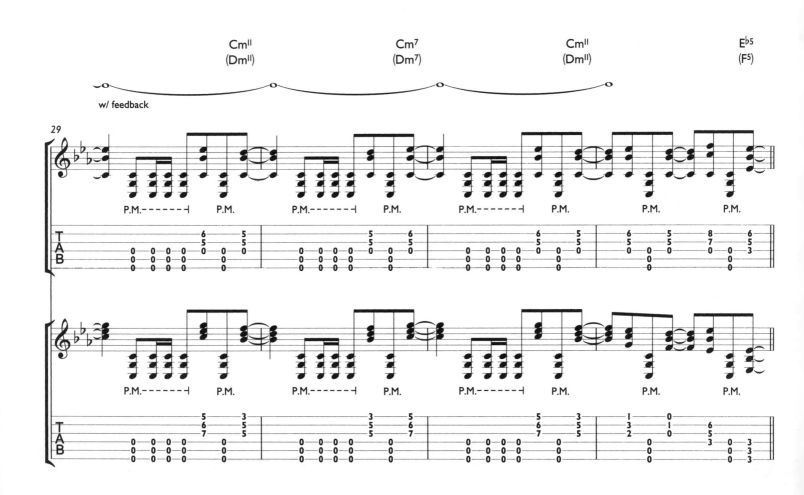

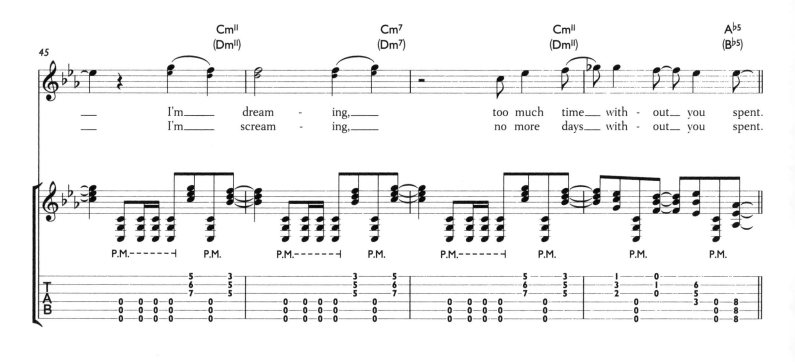

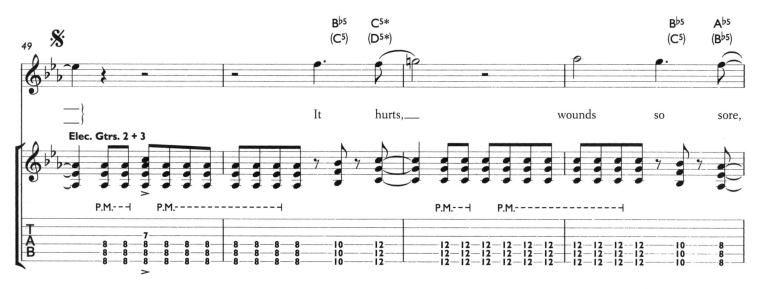

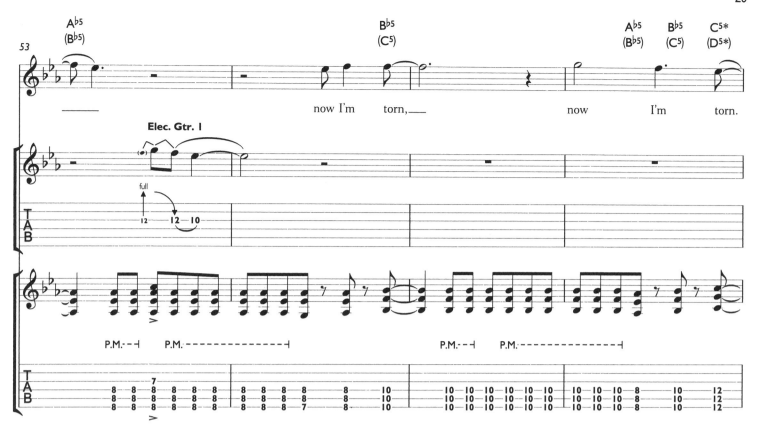

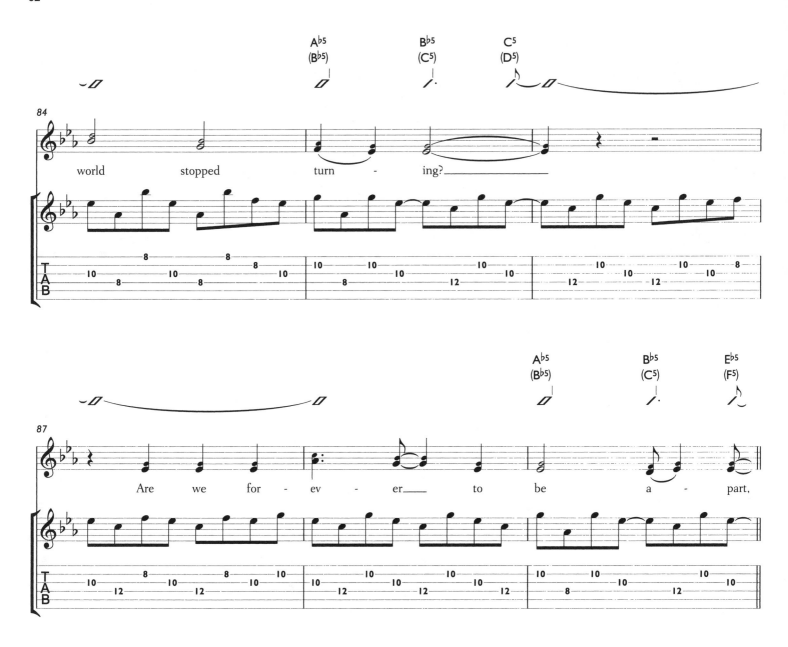

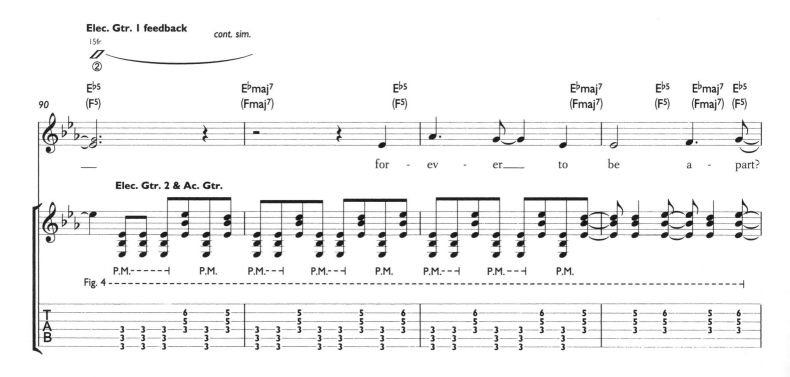

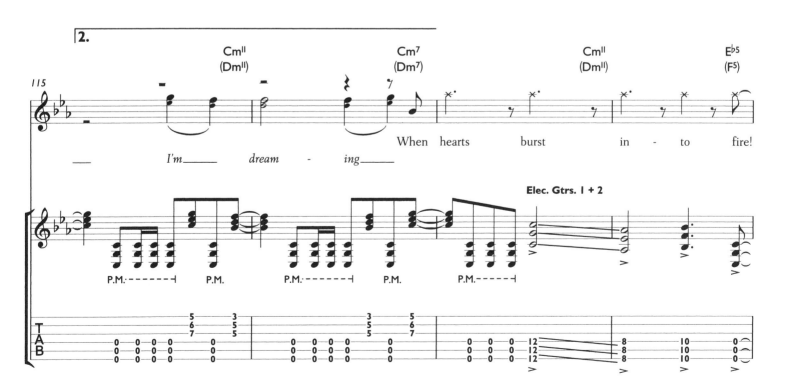

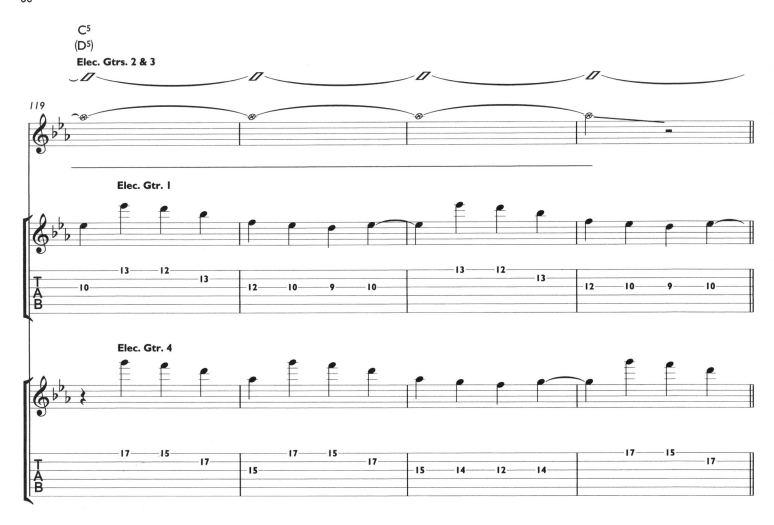

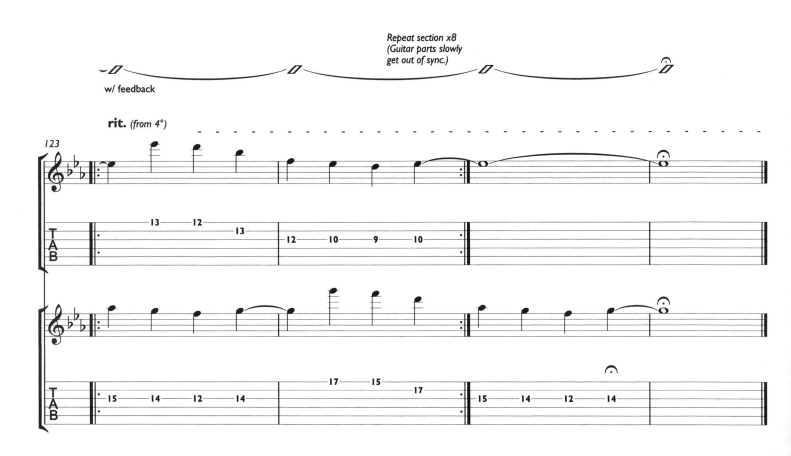

WAKING THE DEMON

Words and Music by Matthew Tuck, Jason James,
Michael Paget and Michael Thomas

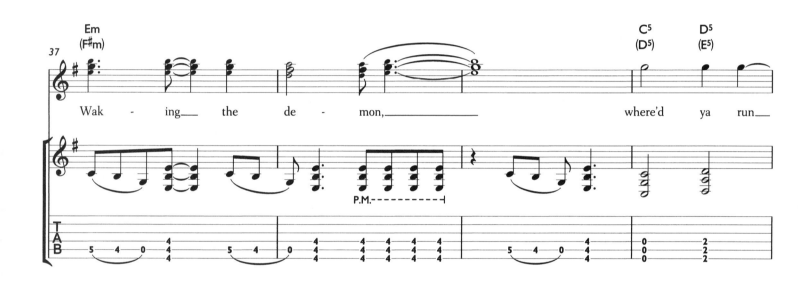

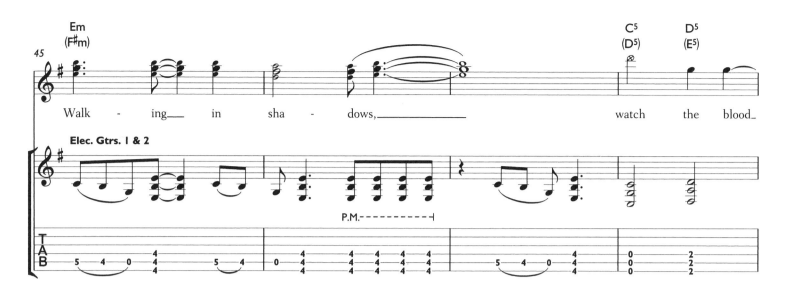

Em (F#m)   C5 (D5)   D5 (E5)

Walk - ing— in sha - dows,———— watch the blood—

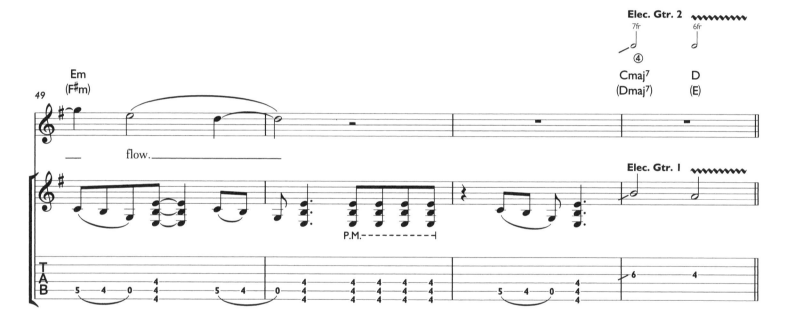

Em (F#m)   Cmaj7 (Dmaj7)   D (E)

— flow.————————

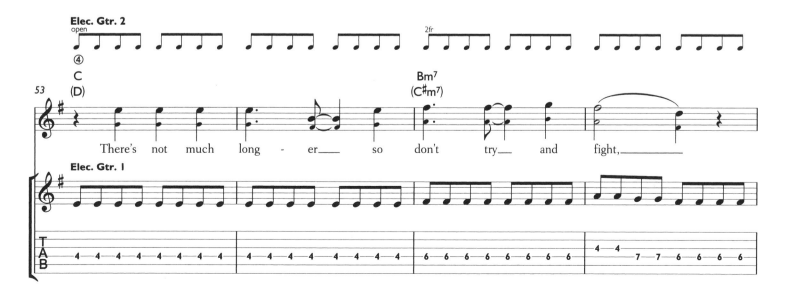

C (D)   Bm7 (C#m7)

There's not much long - er— so don't try— and fight,————

pos - se - sion tak - ing ov - er.   ov - er.

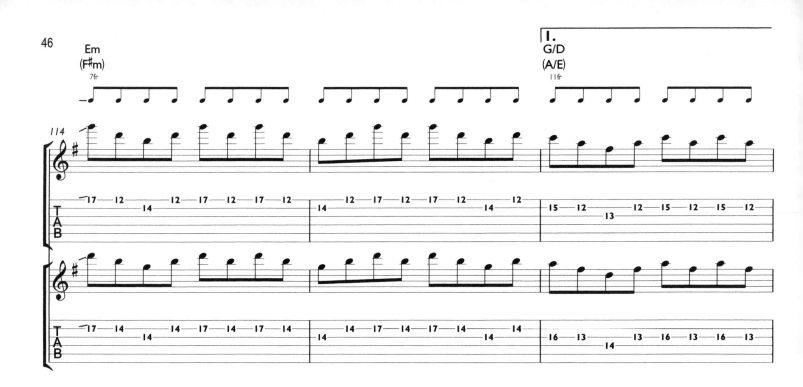

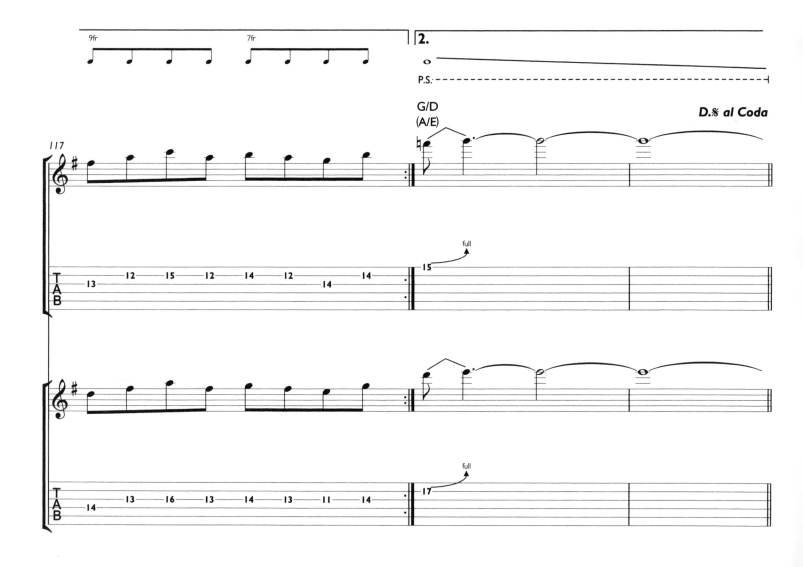

DISAPPEAR

Words and Music by Matthew Tuck, Jason James,
Michael Paget and Michael Thomas

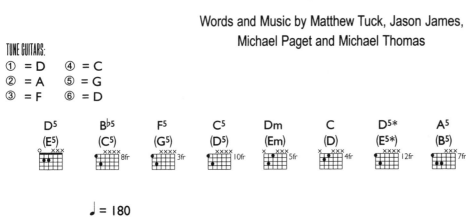

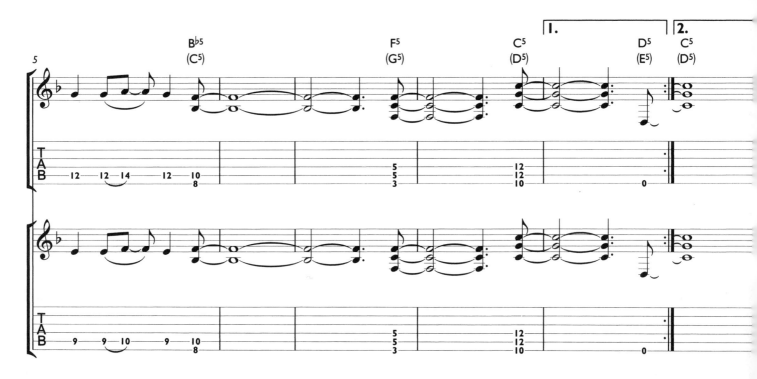

1. Once a - gain_____ the same__ things on_____ your mind,
2. Try to fight,_____ you on - ly make___ things worse,

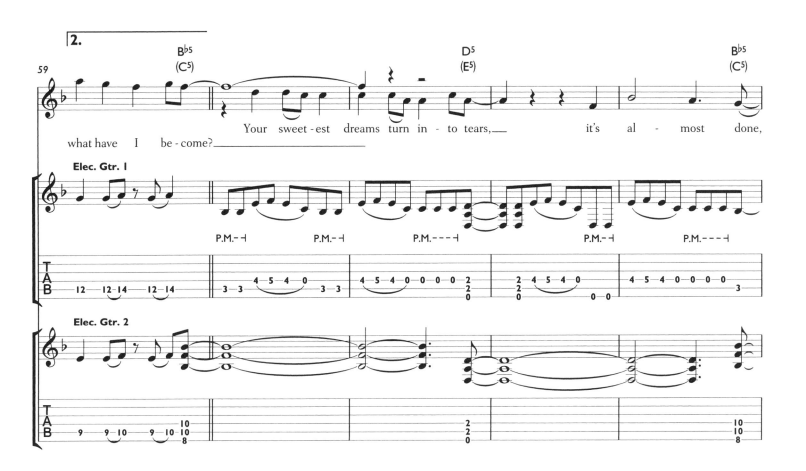

54

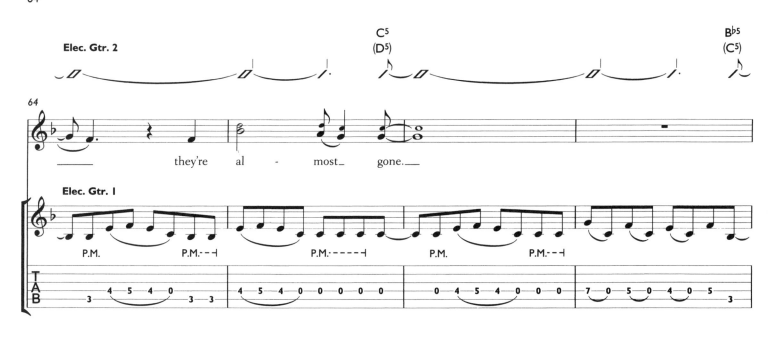

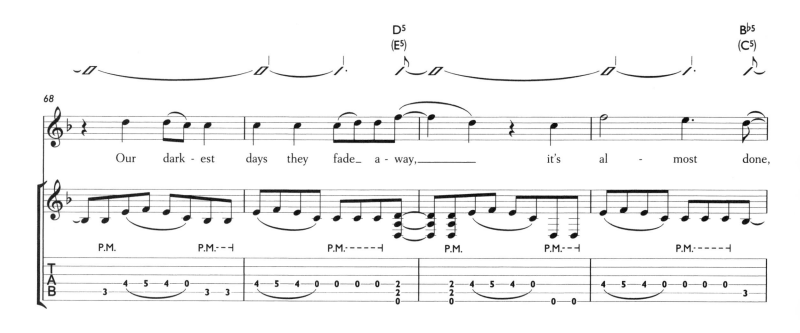

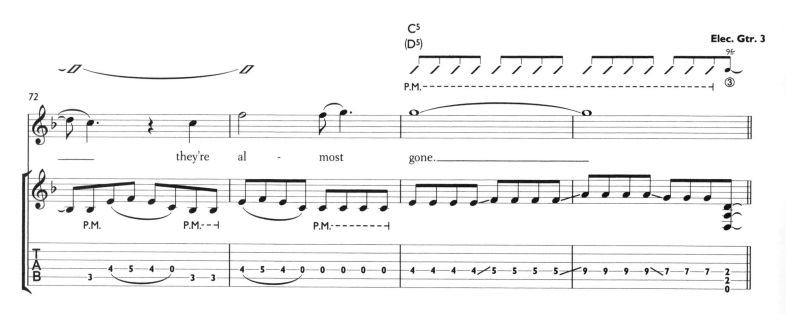

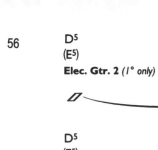

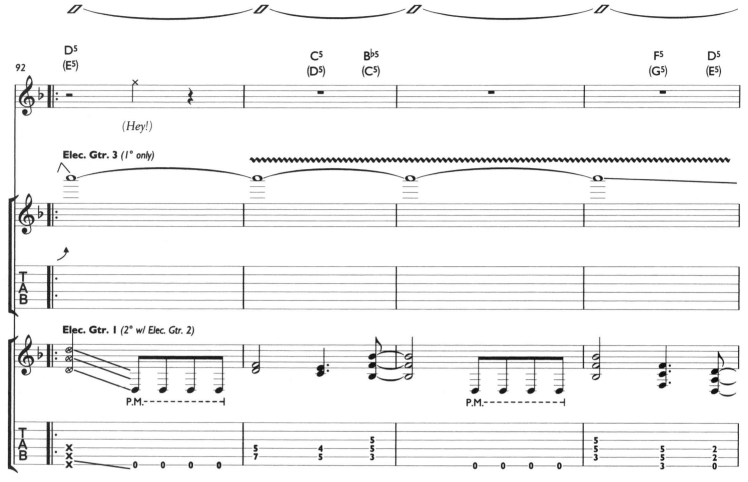

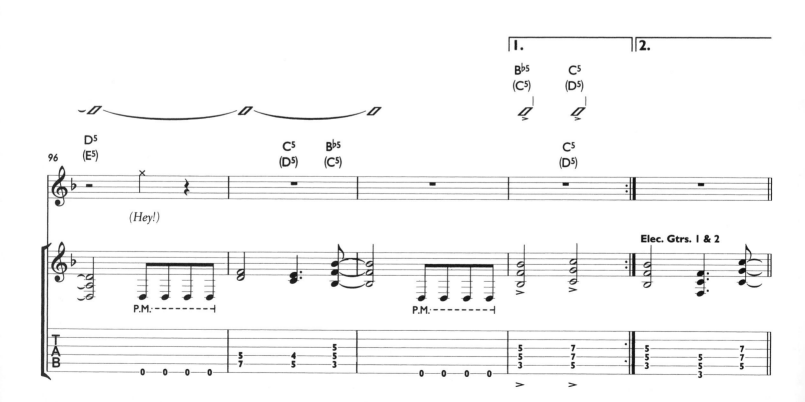

So what's wrong tough guy, why the tears?

You drove me to this, now you dis - ap - pear.

So what's wrong tough guy, why the tears?

You drove me to___ this, now you dis - ap - pear._____

✛ **Coda**

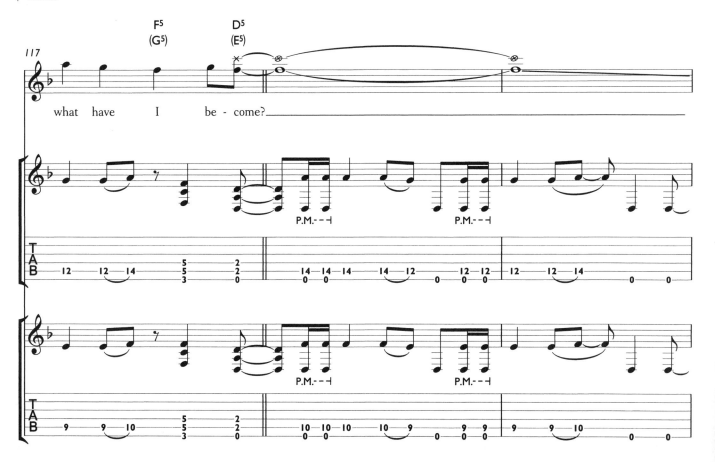

what have I be - come?_____

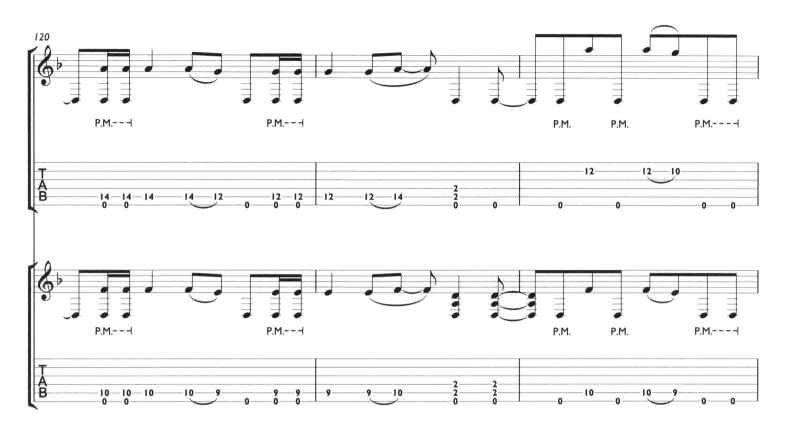

DELIVER US FROM EVIL

Words and Music by Matthew Tuck, Jason James,
Michael Paget and Michael Thomas

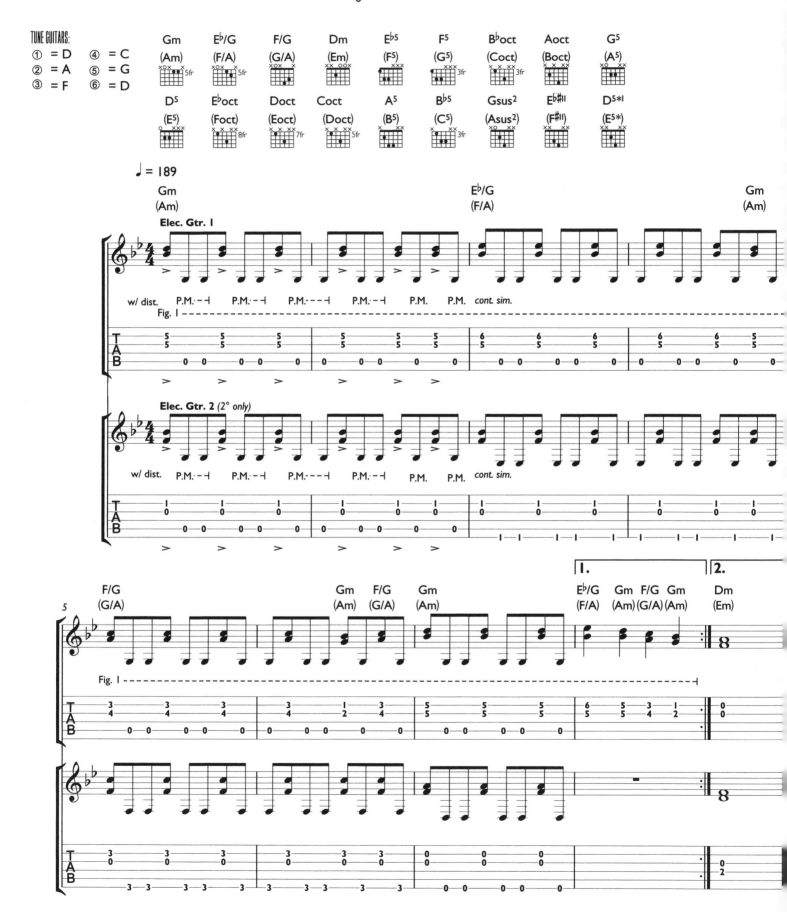

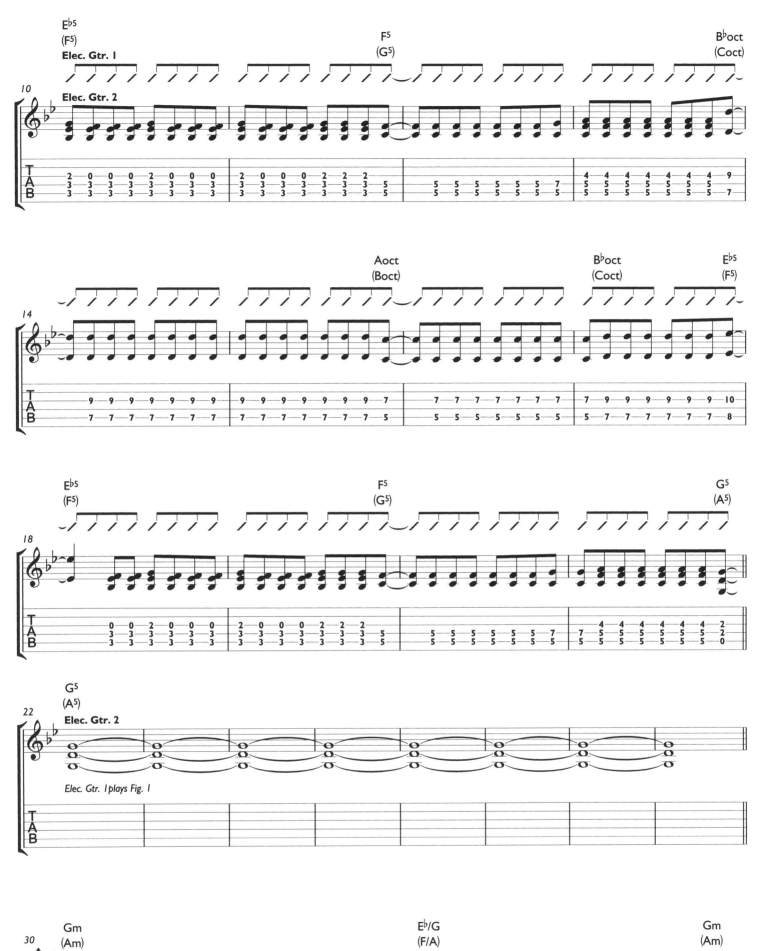

1. What's hap-pen-ing___ to me?___ I'm dy-ing from the

Elec. Gtrs. 1 + 2 play Fig. 1

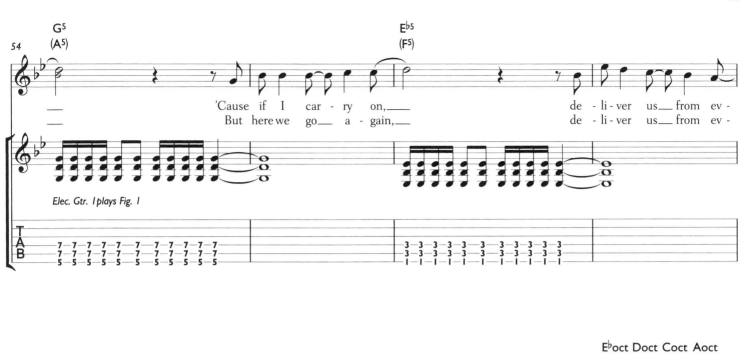

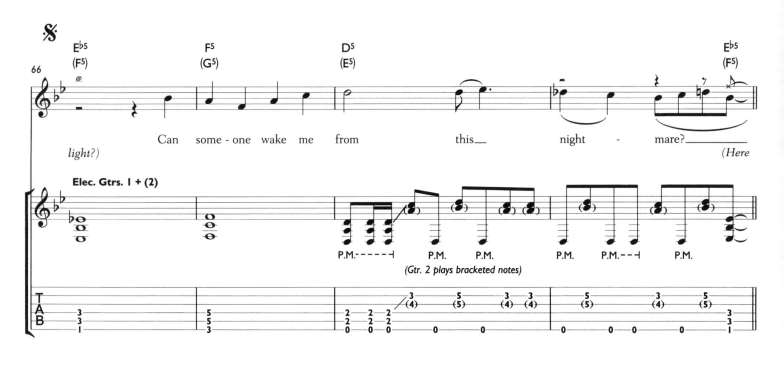

Can some-one wake me from this___ night - mare?_____ (Here
light?)

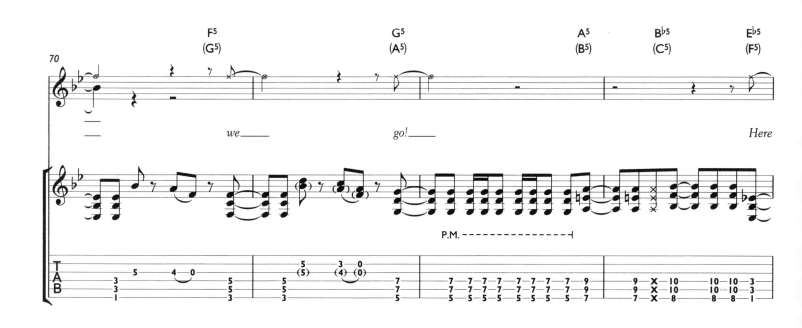

we_____ go!_____ Here

To Coda ✛

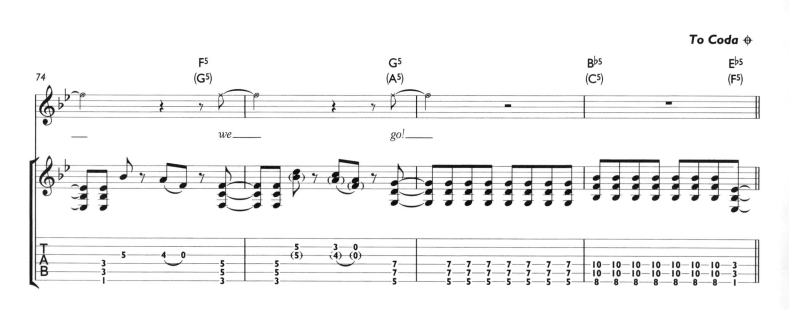

we_____ go!_____

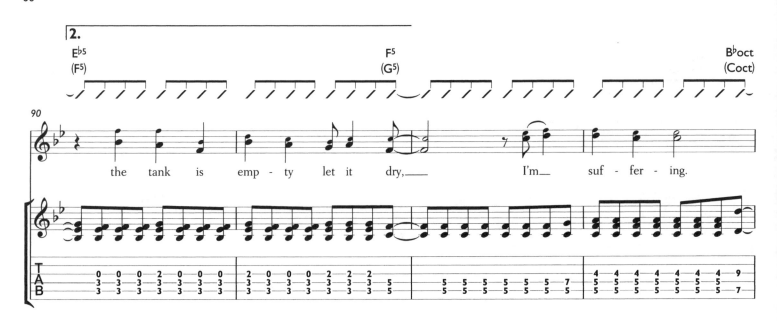

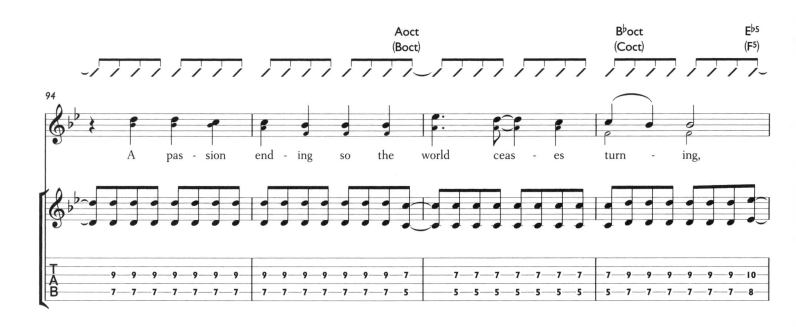

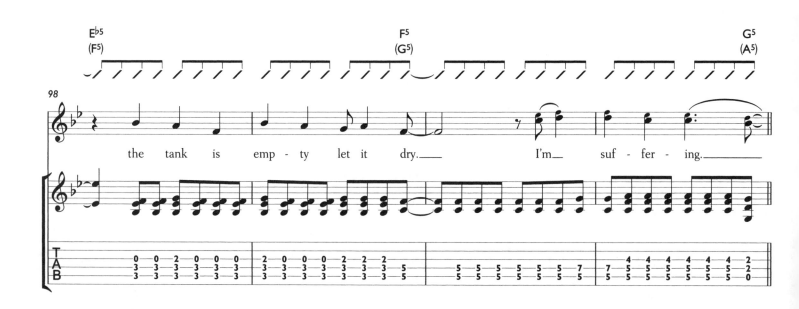

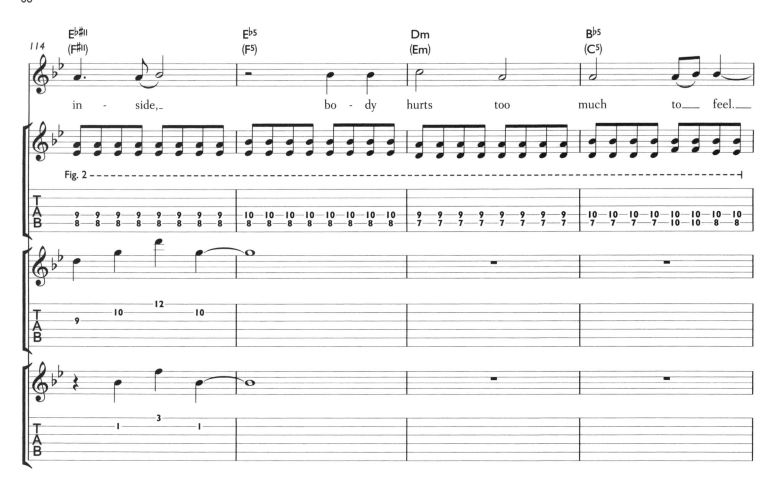

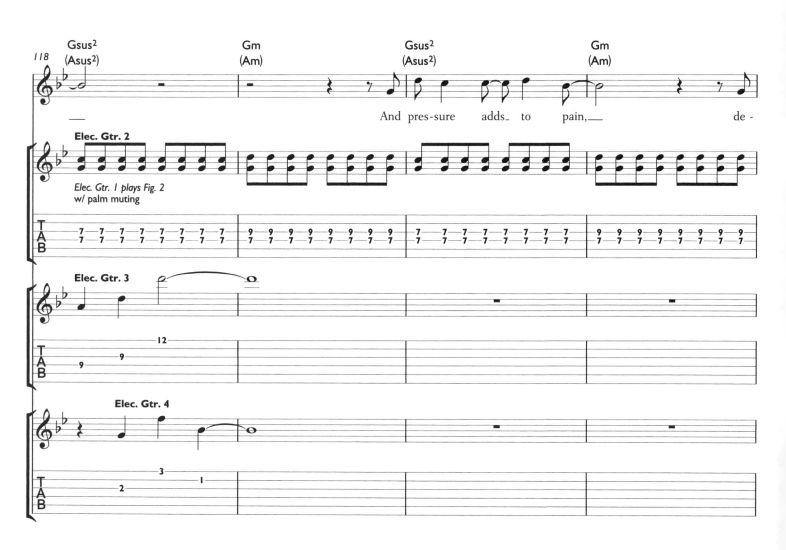

we're ev - il, we're ev - il, we're ev - il.

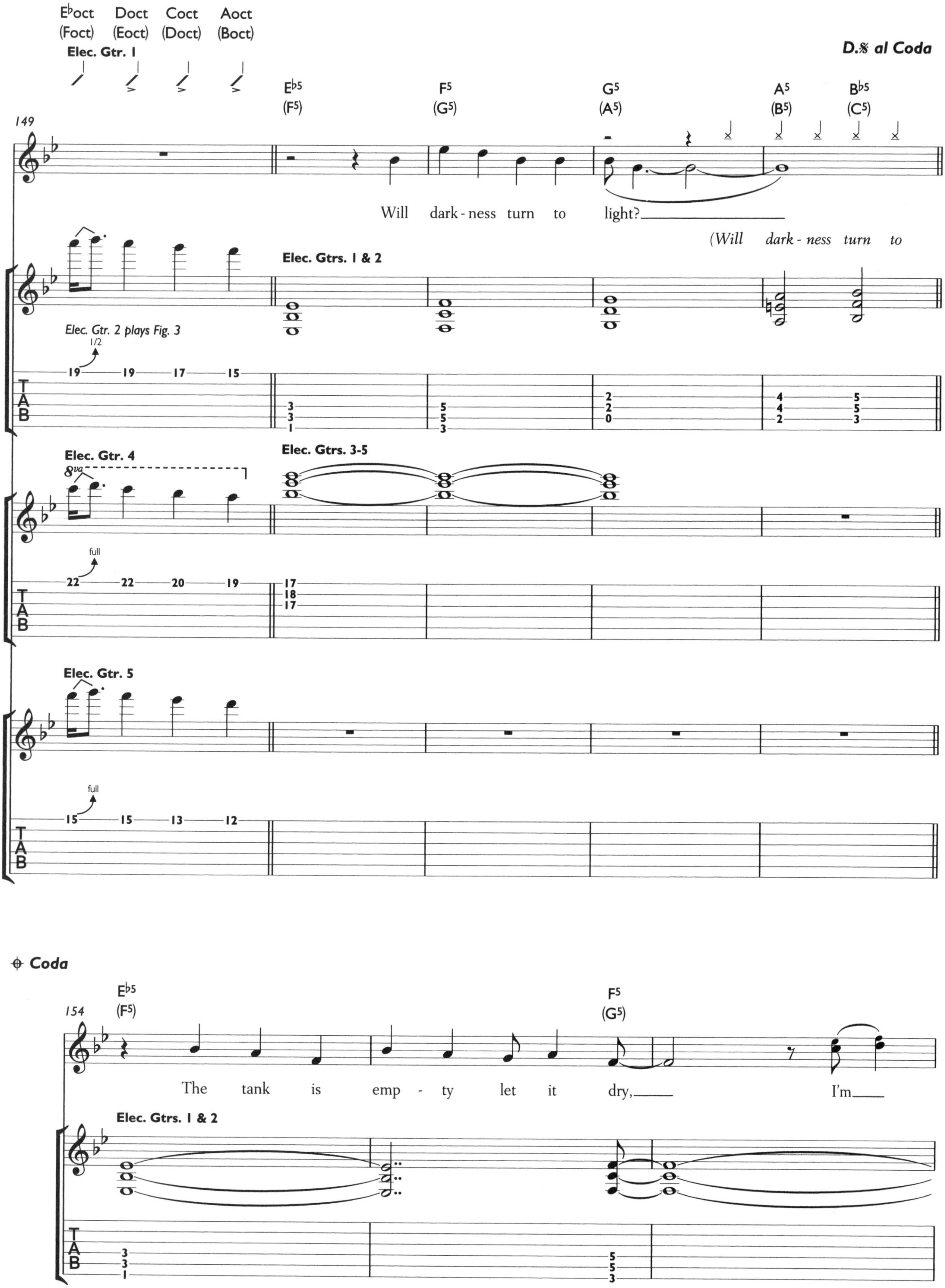
E♭oct Doct Coct Aoct
(Foct) (Eoct) (Doct) (Boct)
Elec. Gtr. 1
D.𝄋 al Coda
E♭5 (F5) F5 (G5) G5 (A5) A5 (B5) B♭5 (C5)
149
Will dark - ness turn to light?
(Will dark - ness turn to
Elec. Gtrs. 1 & 2
Elec. Gtr. 2 plays Fig. 3
1/2
Elec. Gtr. 4
8va
full
Elec. Gtrs. 3-5
Elec. Gtr. 5
full
Coda
E♭5 (F5) F5 (G5)
154
The tank is emp - ty let it dry, I'm
Elec. Gtrs. 1 & 2

TAKE IT OUT ON ME

Words by Matthew Tuck and Benji Webbe
Music by Matthew Tuck, Jason James, Michael Paget and Michael Thomas

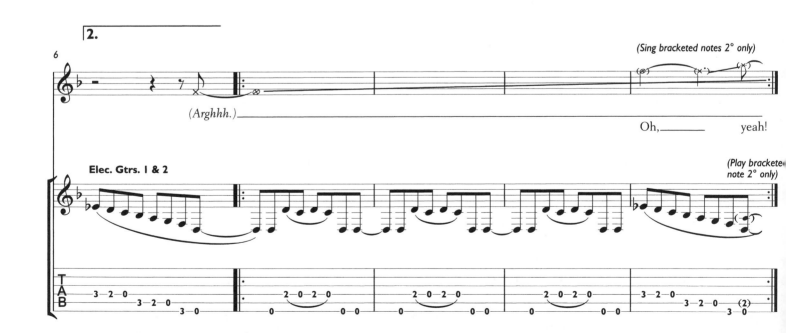

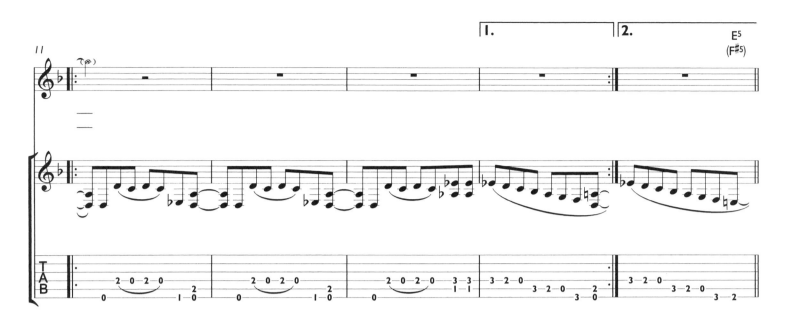

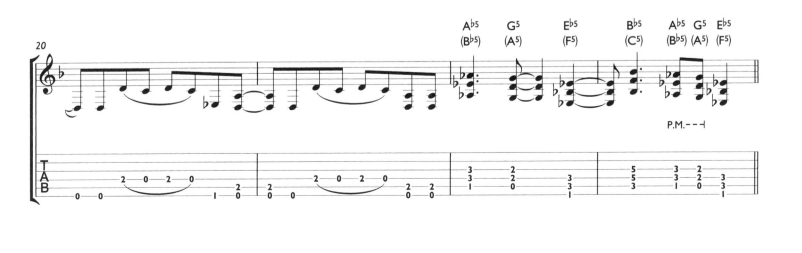

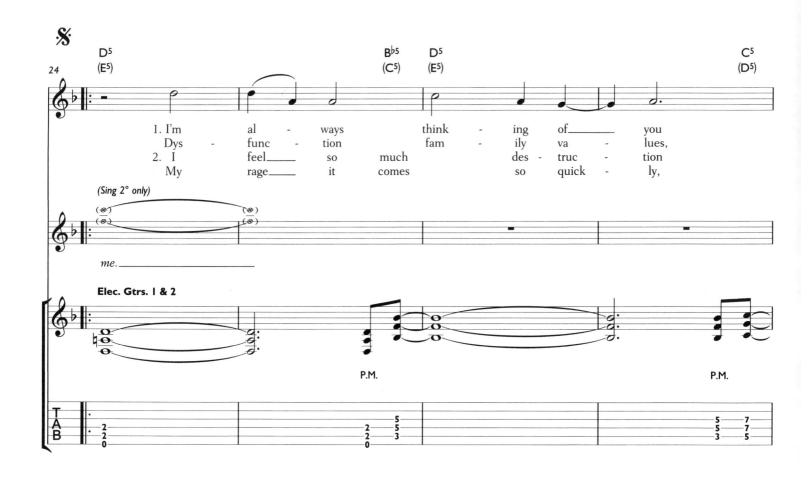

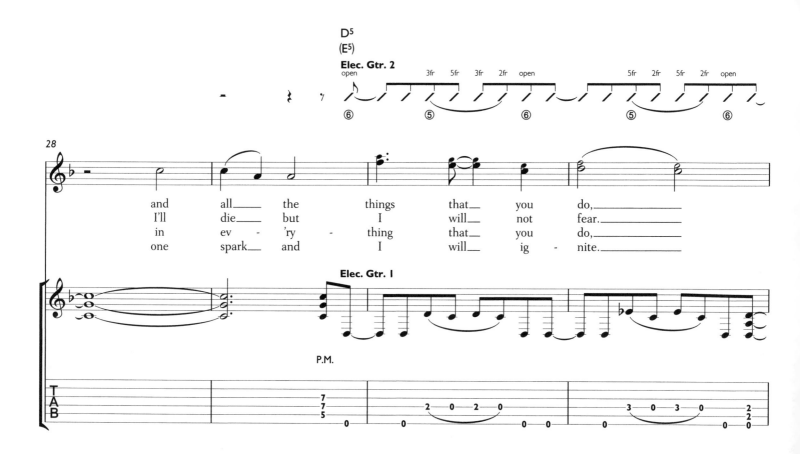

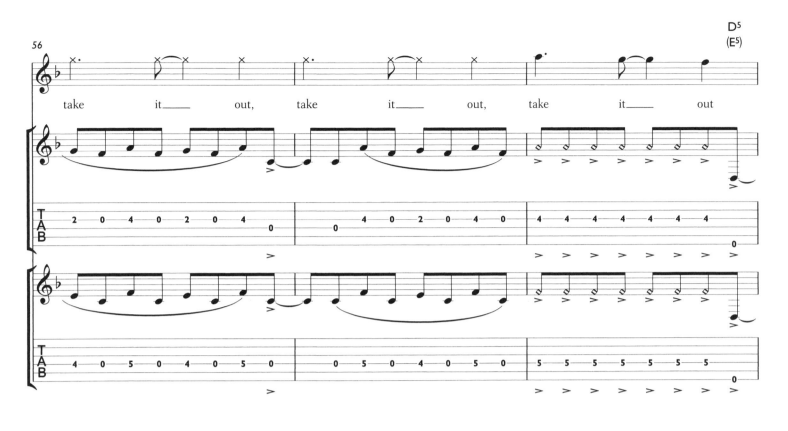

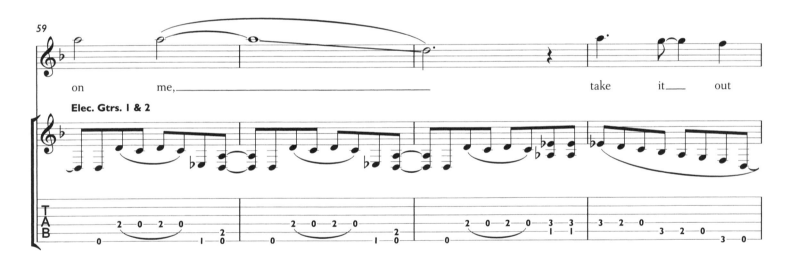

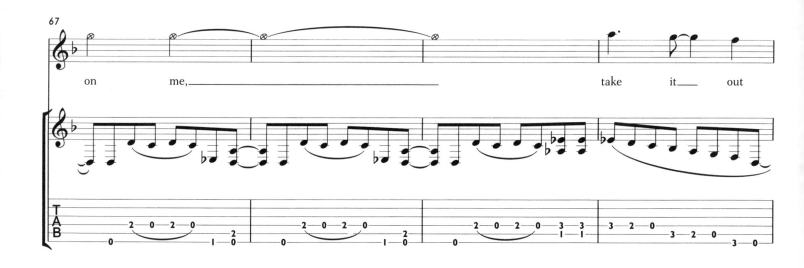

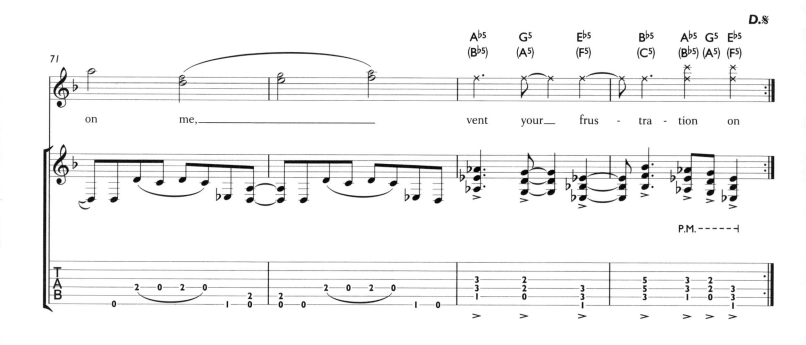

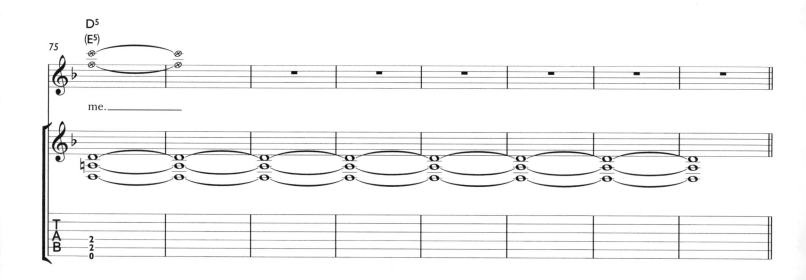

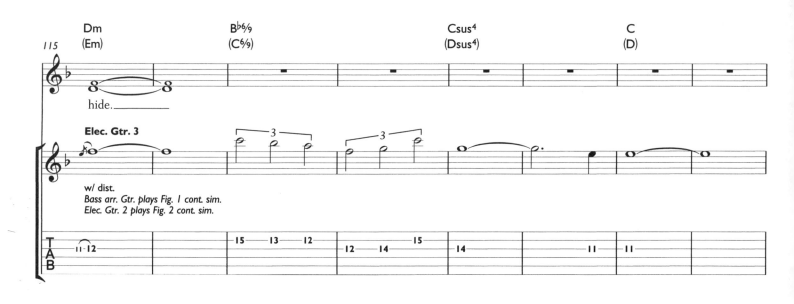

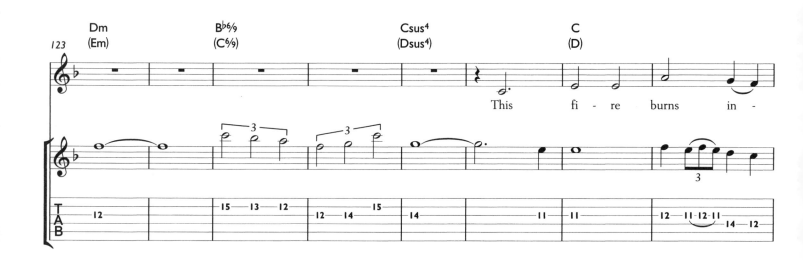

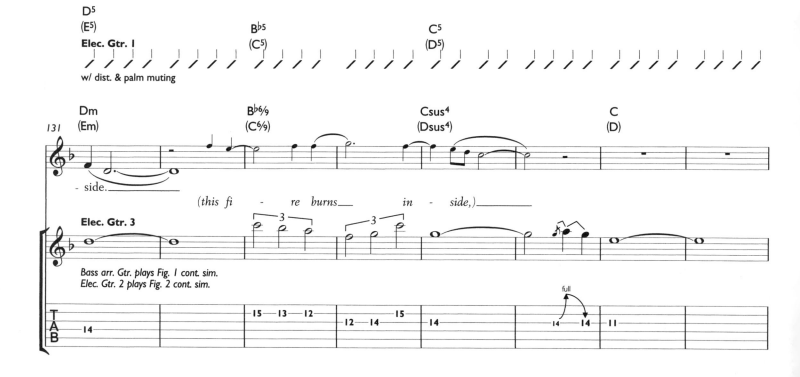

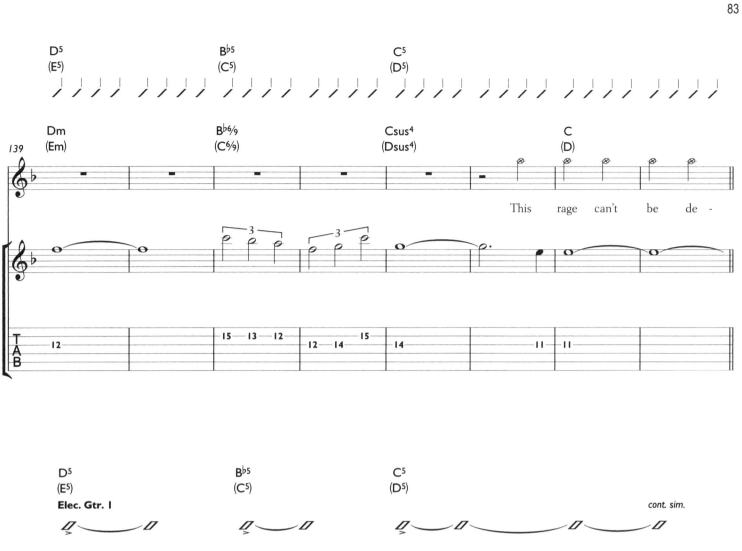

Lyrics: This rage can't be de-

Lyrics: - nied!_____

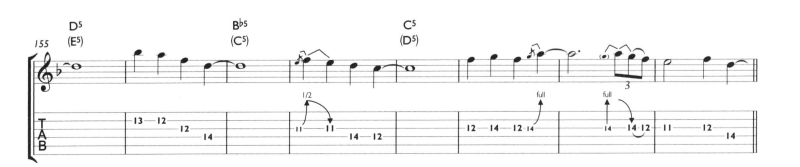

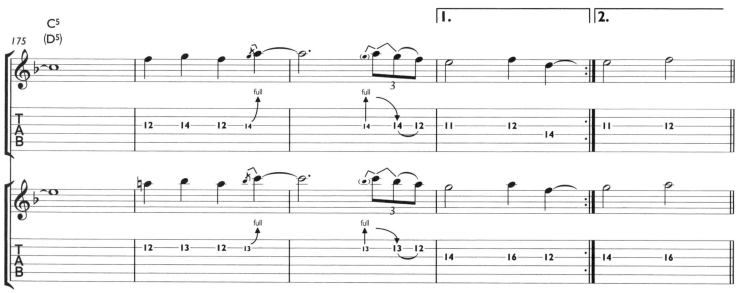

D.𝄌 al Coda

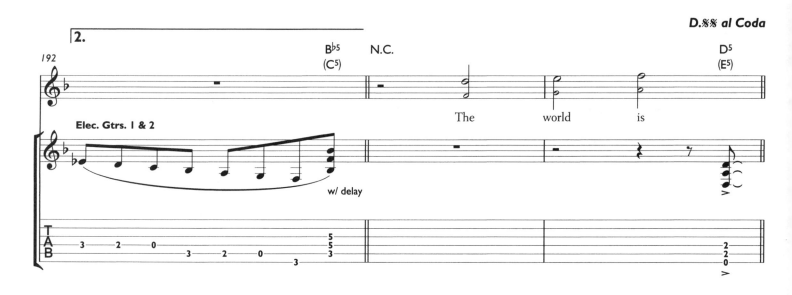

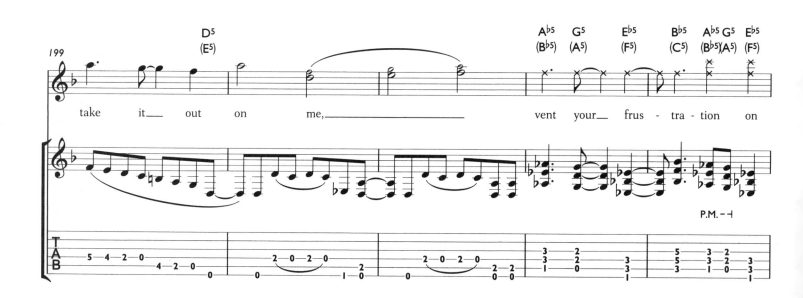

SAY GOODNIGHT

Words and Music by Matthew Tuck, Jason James,
Michael Paget and Michael Thomas

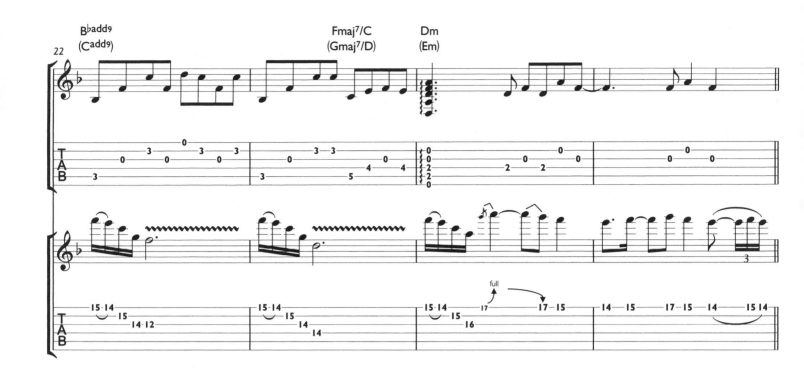

Elec. Gtr. 2

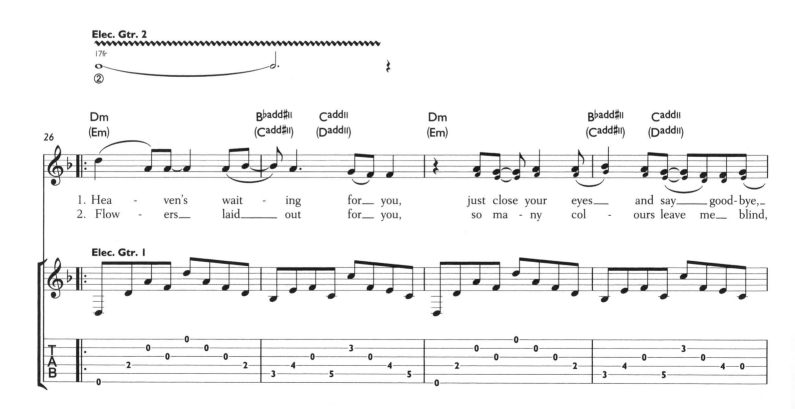

1. Hea - ven's wait - ing for__ you, just close your eyes__ and say__ good-bye,__
2. Flow - ers__ laid__ out for__ you, so ma - ny col - ours leave me__ blind,

Elec. Gtr. 1

No breath left___ in-side of me,___ shat-tered glass keeps fall - ing.___

Say good - night,_____ just sleep
(Say_____ good - night,_____ just sleep

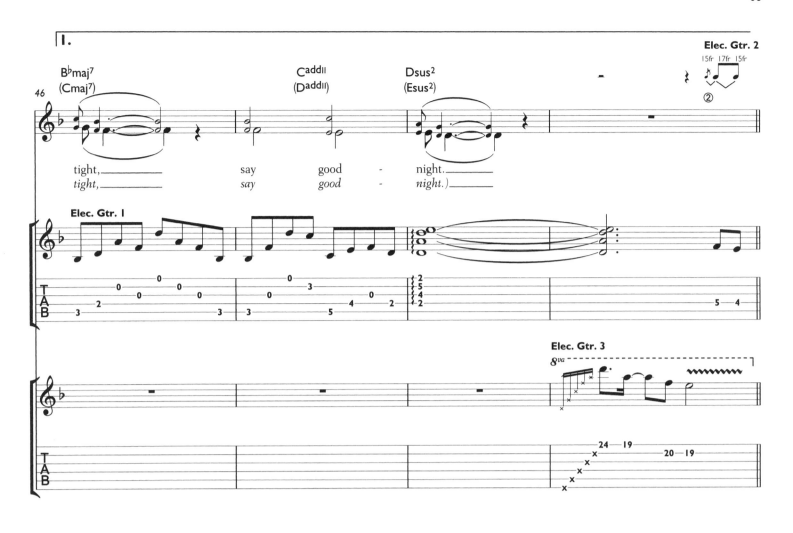

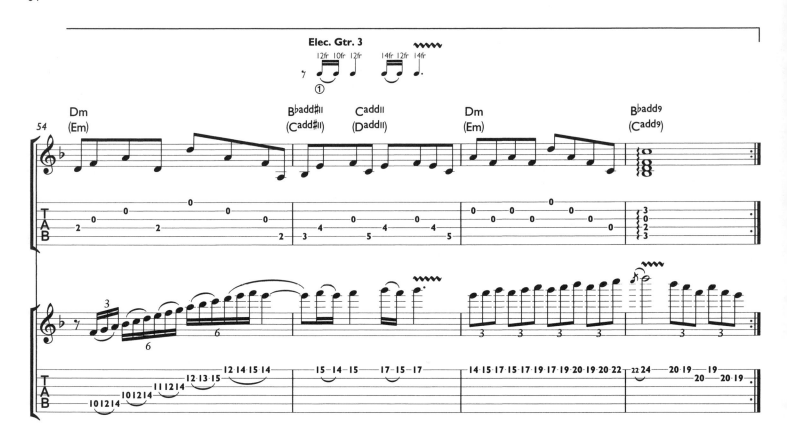

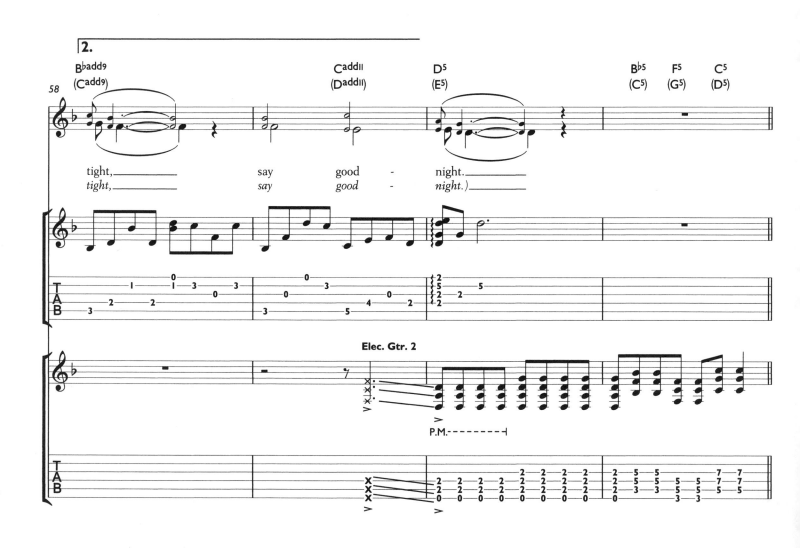

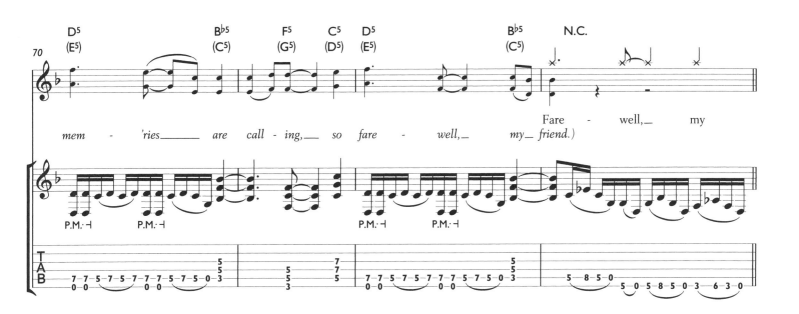

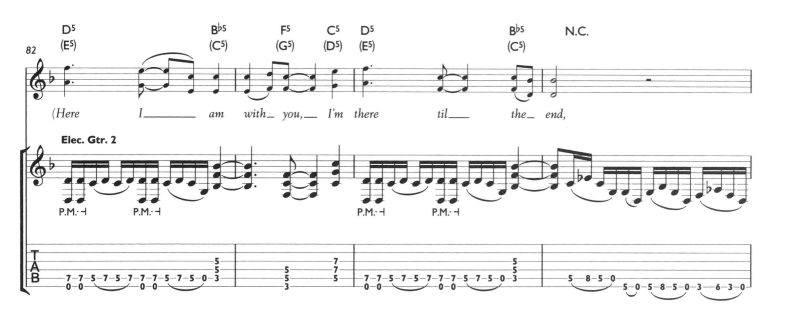

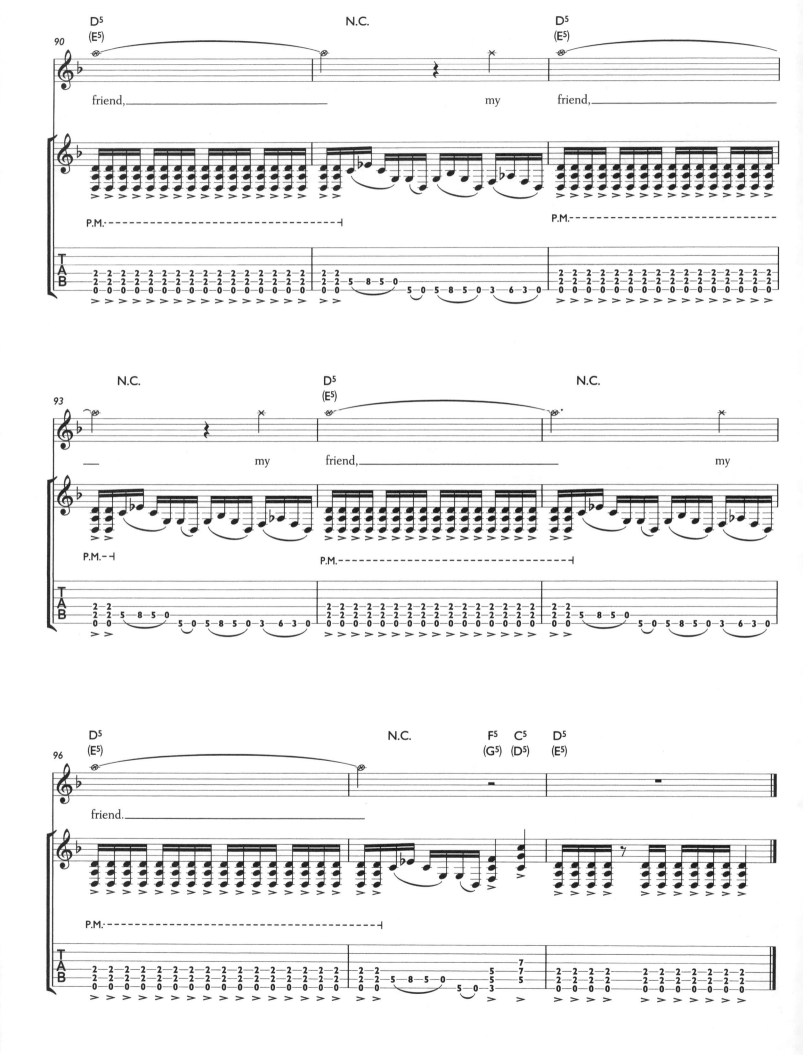

END OF DAYS

Words and Music by Matthew Tuck, Jason James,
Michael Paget and Michael Thomas

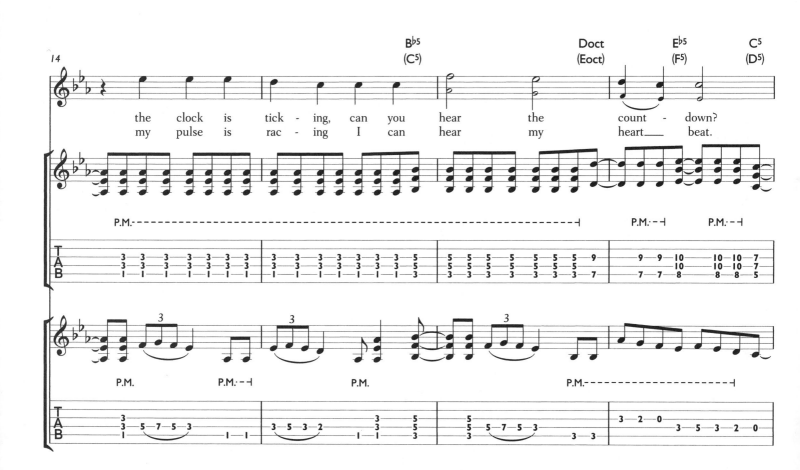

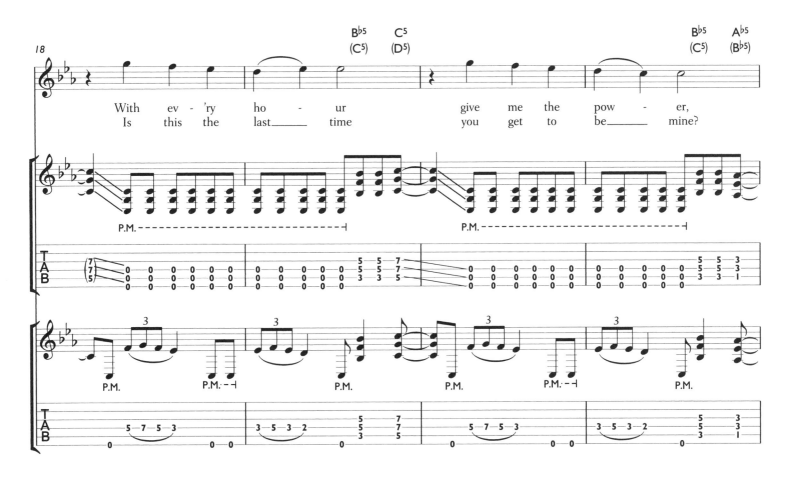

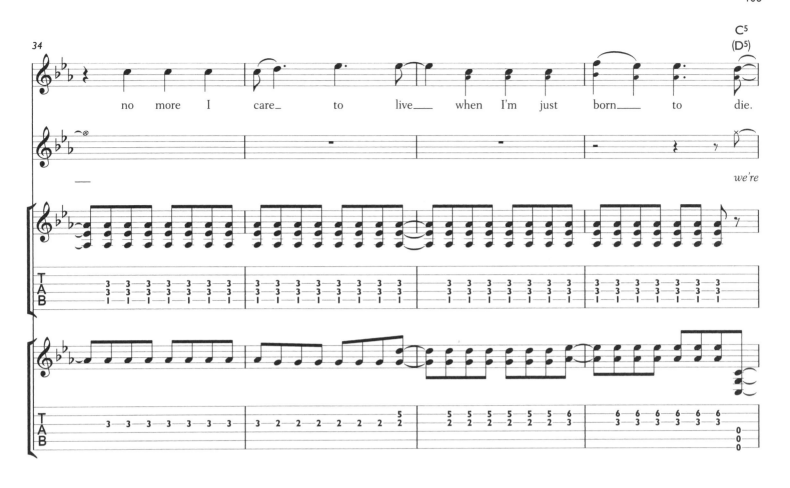
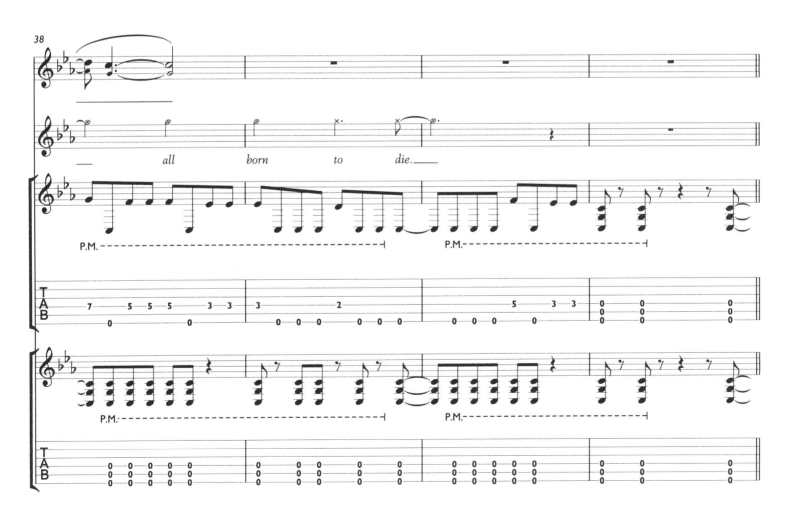

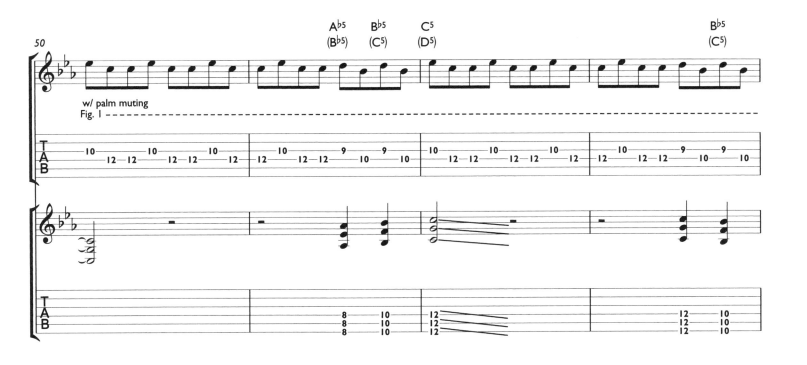

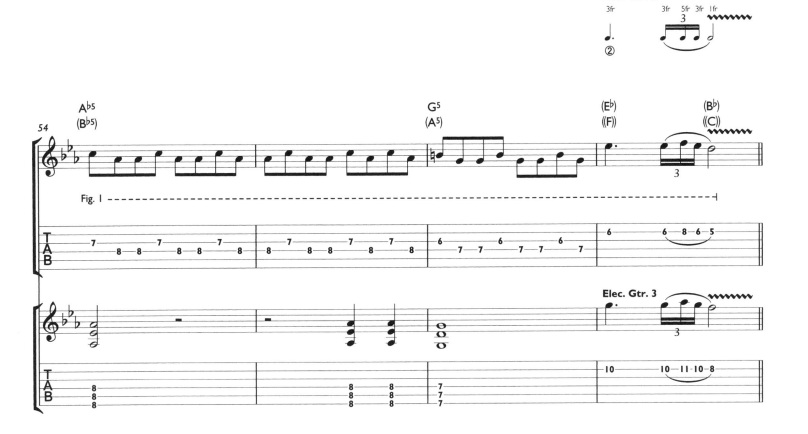

No more sor - rows, no to - mor - rows,_____

Elec. Gtr. 3

w/ palm muting
Fig. 2 ---
Elec. Gtr. 1 plays Fig. 1

Elec. Gtr. 2

w/ palm muting

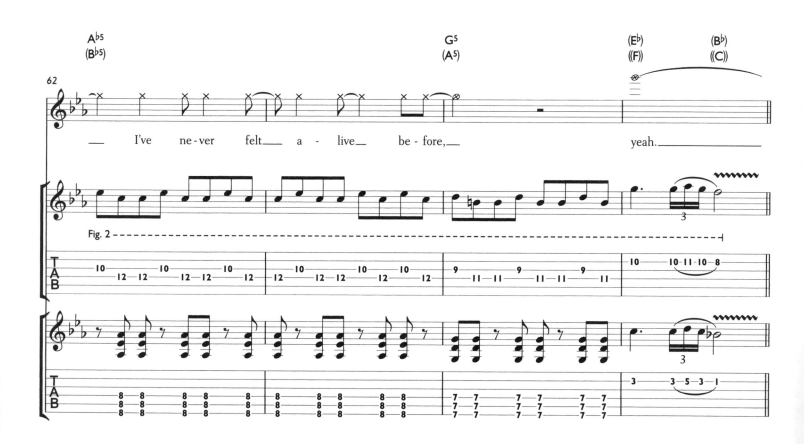

_____ I've ne - ver felt___ a - live___ be - fore,___ yeah._____

Fig. 2 --

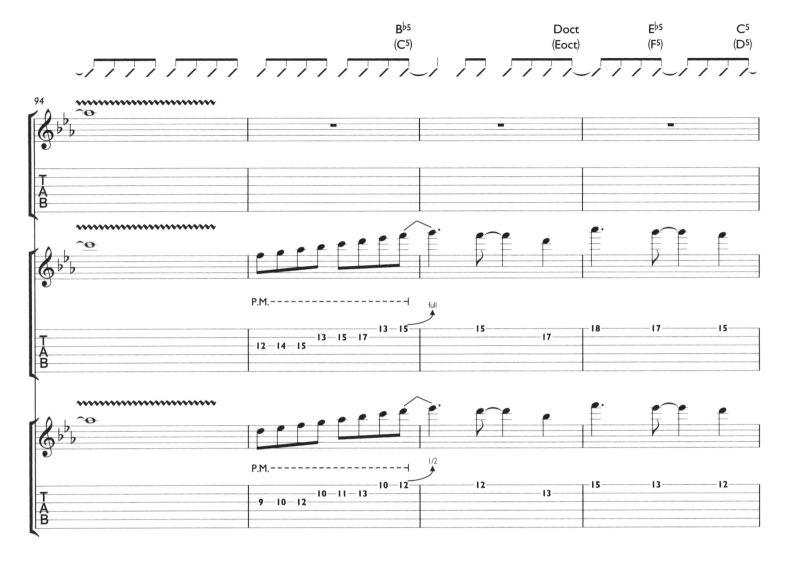

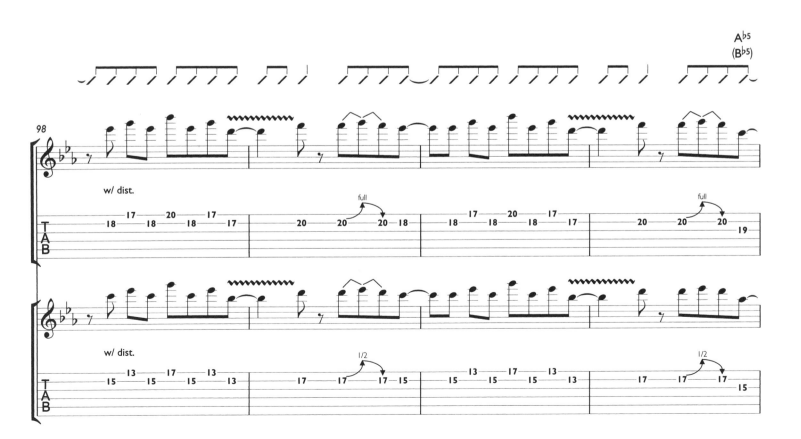

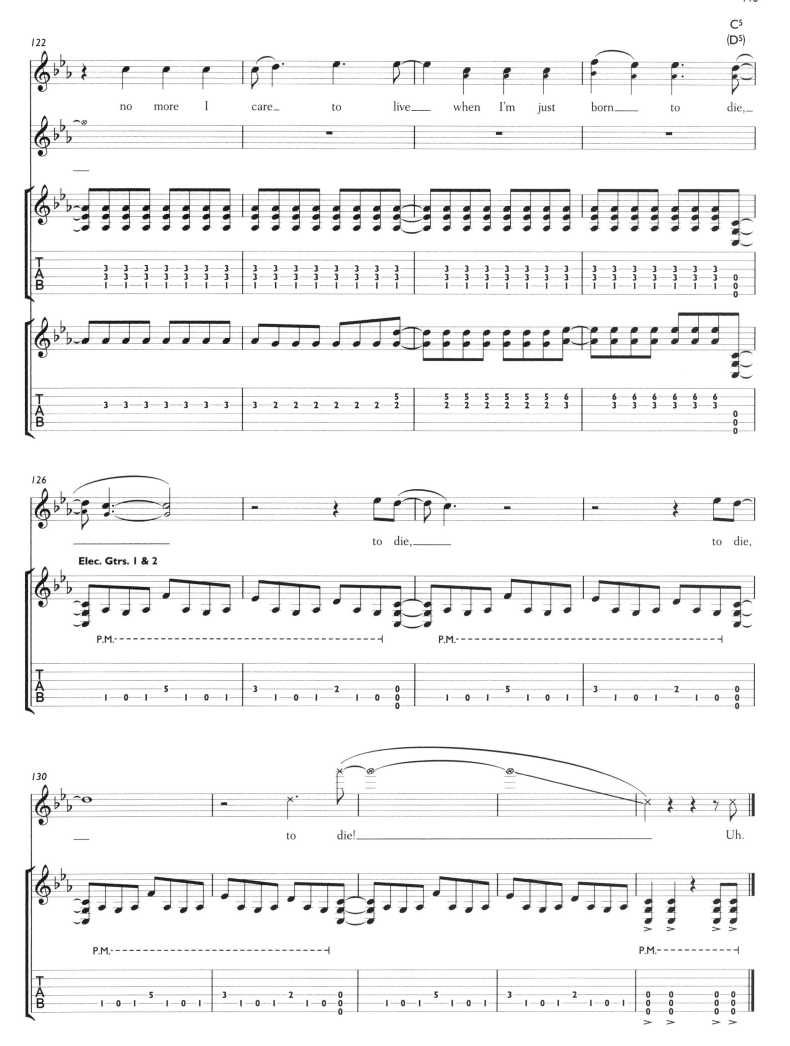

LAST TO KNOW

Words and Music by Matthew Tuck, Jason James,
Michael Paget and Michael Thomas

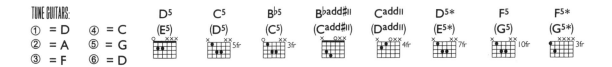

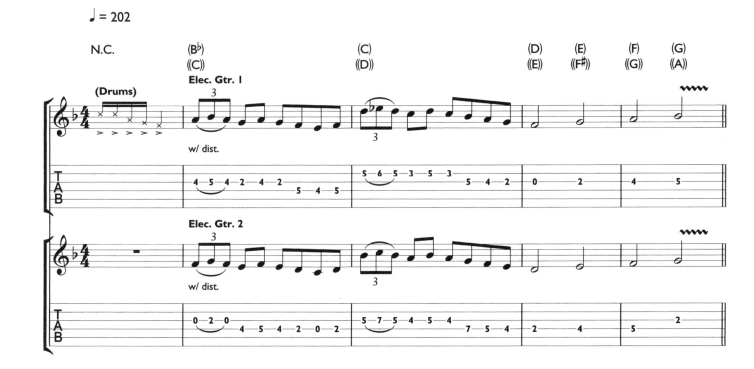

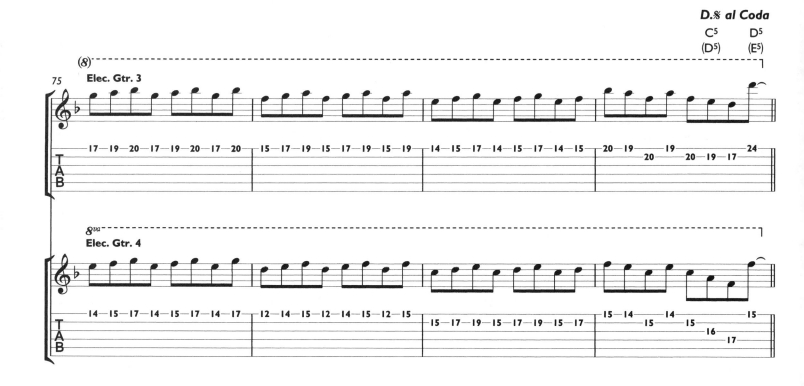

FOREVER AND ALWAYS

Words and Music by Matthew Tuck, Jason James,
Michael Paget and Michael Thomas

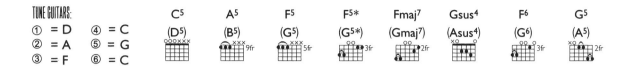

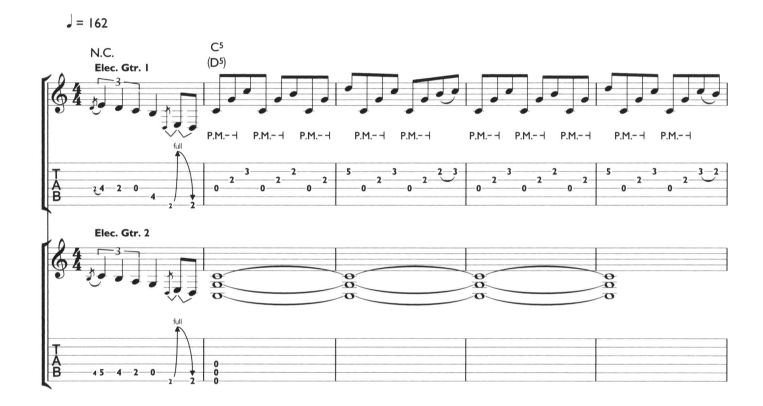

1. That time is here a - gain,____ pre - pare to be a -
2. These days are dead a - gain,____ it's emp - ty from the____

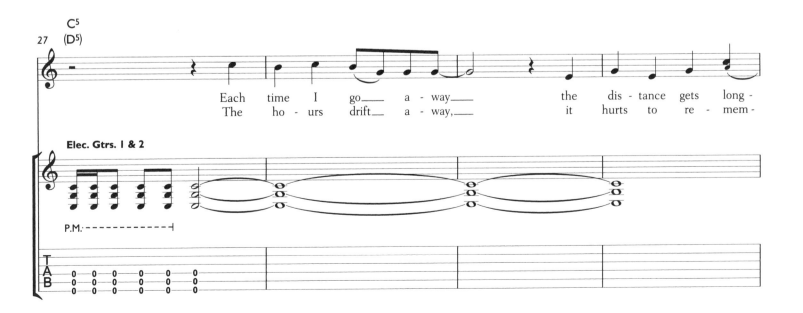

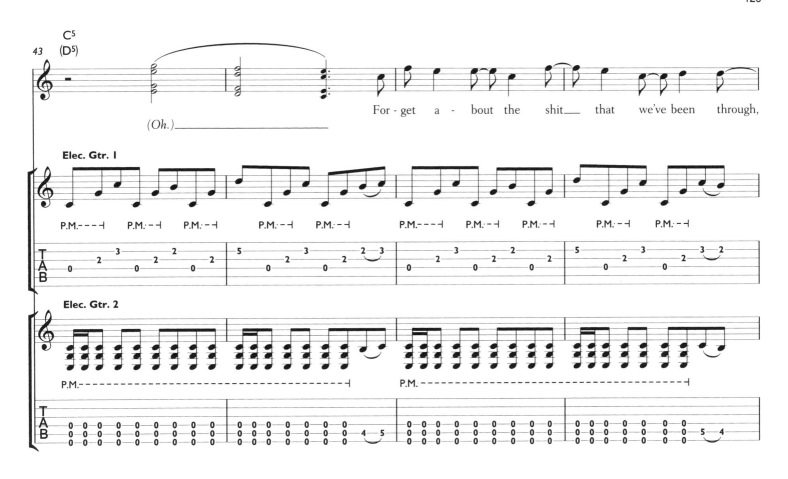

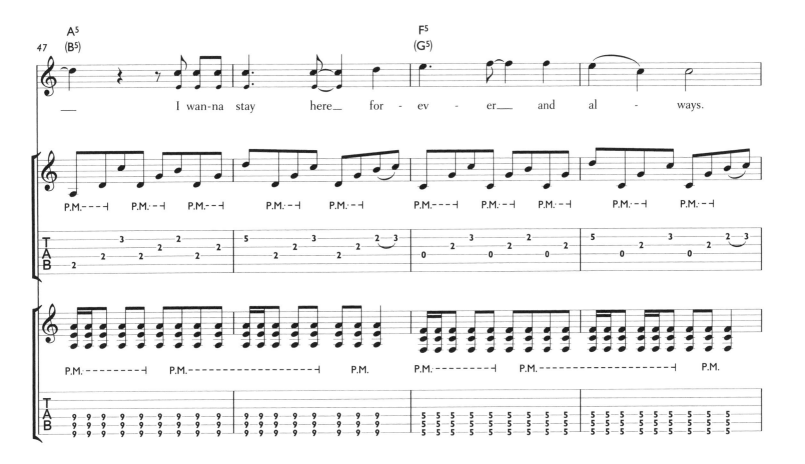

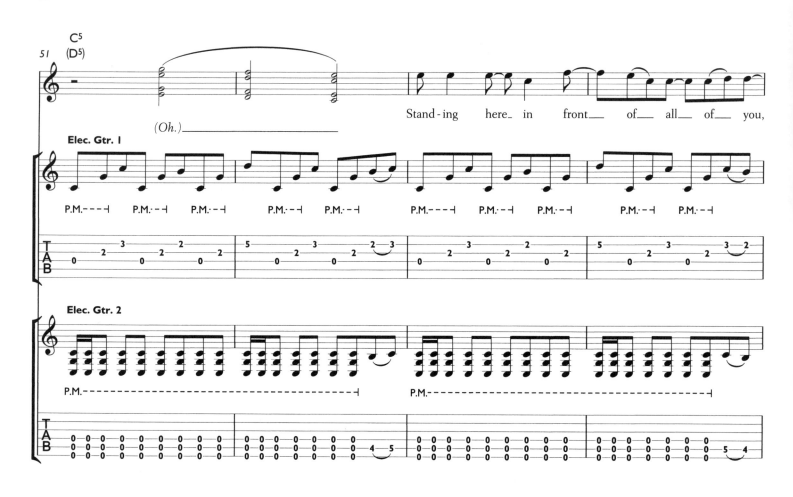

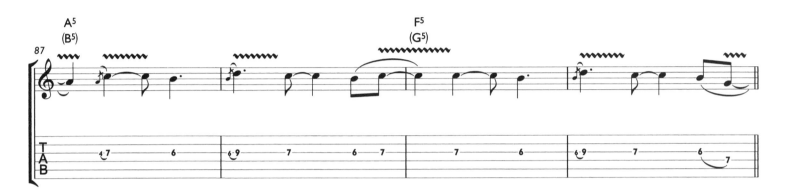

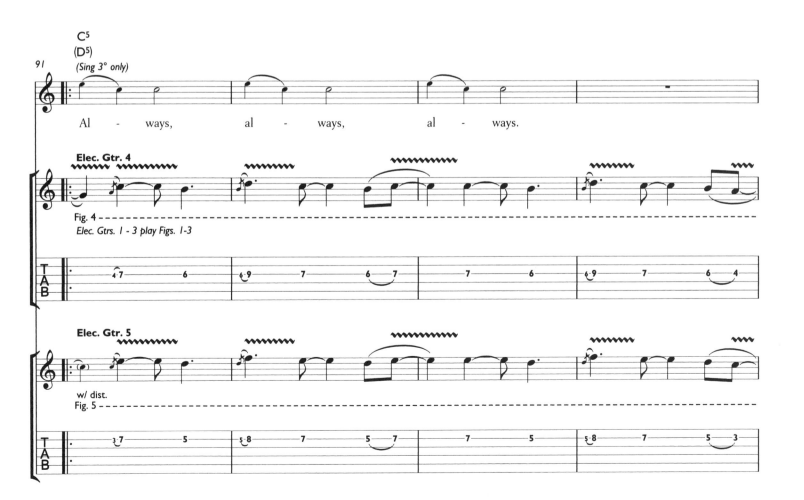

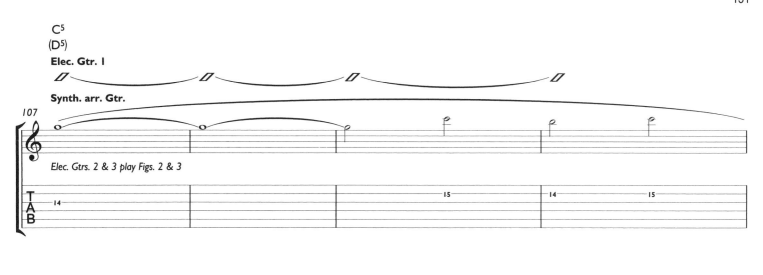

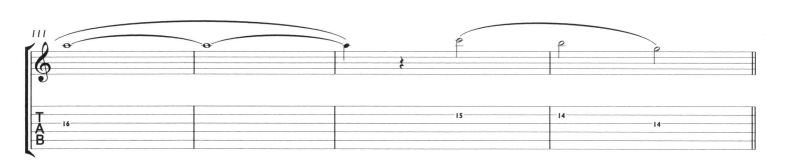

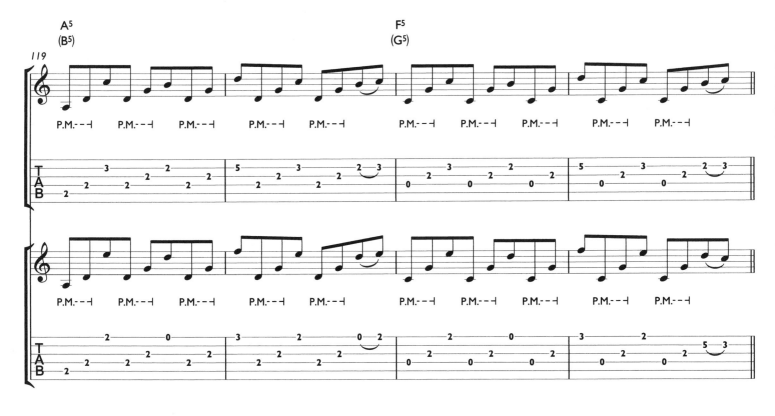

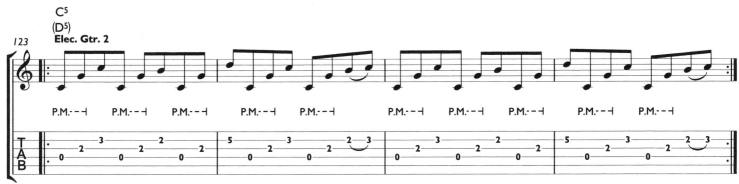

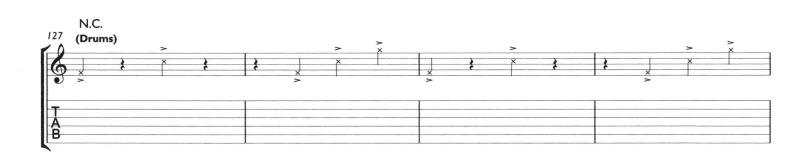

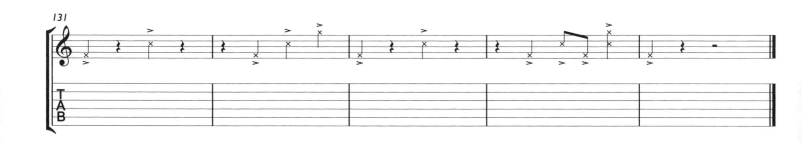

ASHES OF THE INNOCENT

Words and Music by Matthew Tuck, Jason James,
Michael Paget and Michael Thomas

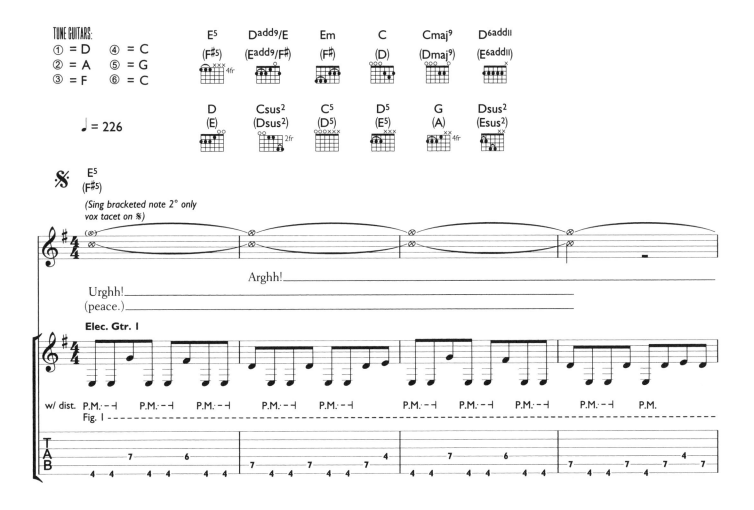

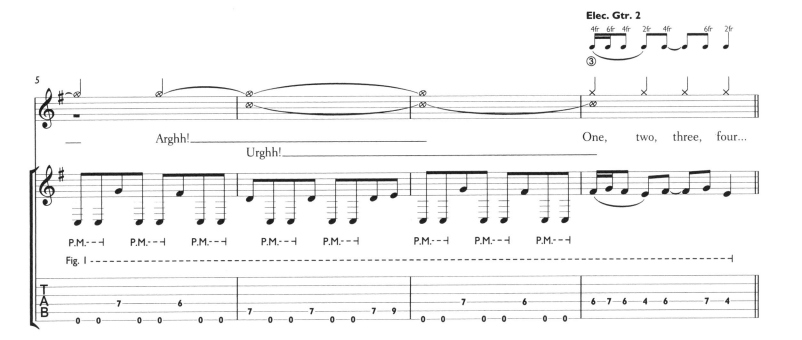

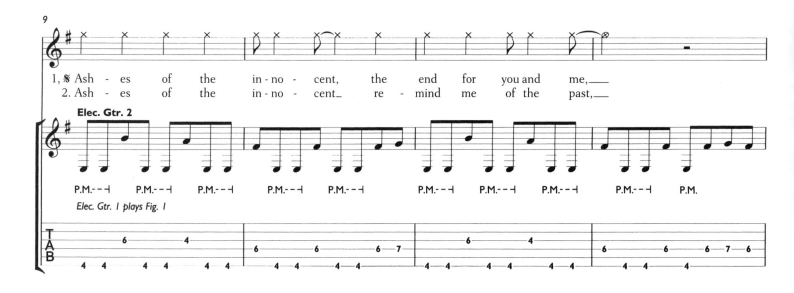

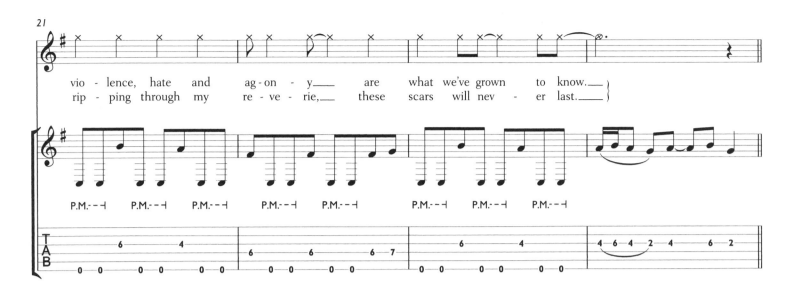

vio - lence, hate and ag - on - y___ are what we've grown to know.___ }
rip - ping through my re - ve - rie,___ these scars will nev - er last.___ }

♩ = 213

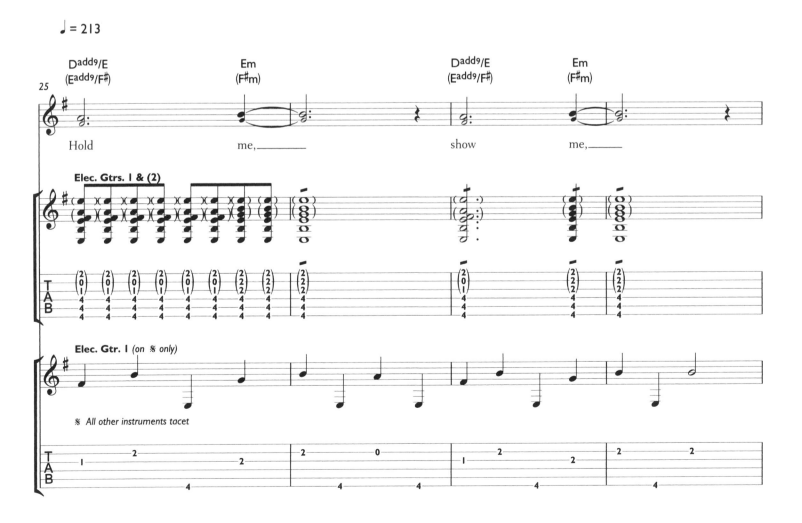

| Dadd9/E | Em | Dadd9/E | Em |
| (Eadd9/F#) | (F#m) | (Eadd9/F#) | (F#m) |

Hold   me,___   show   me,___

Elec. Gtrs. I & (2)

Elec. Gtr. I *(on 𝄋 only)*

𝄋 *All other instruments tacet*

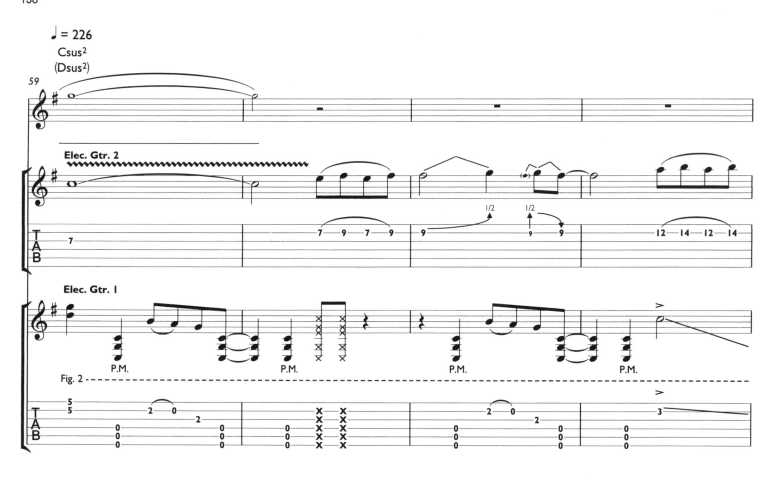

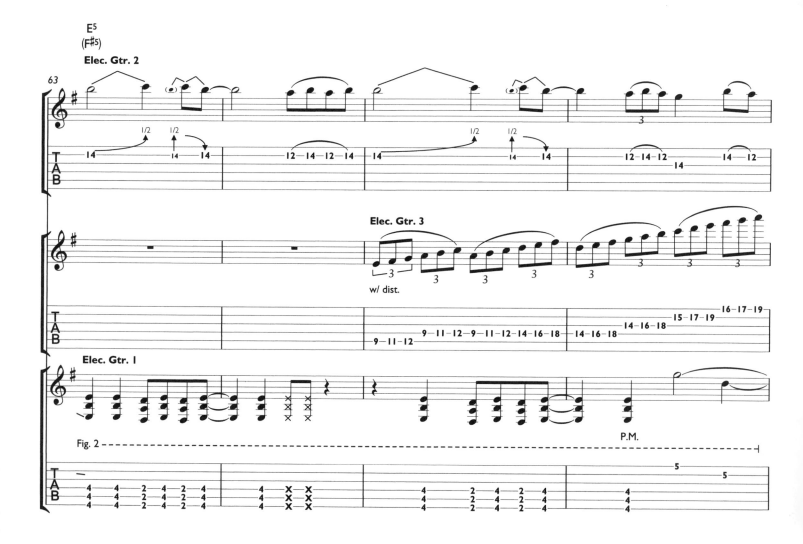

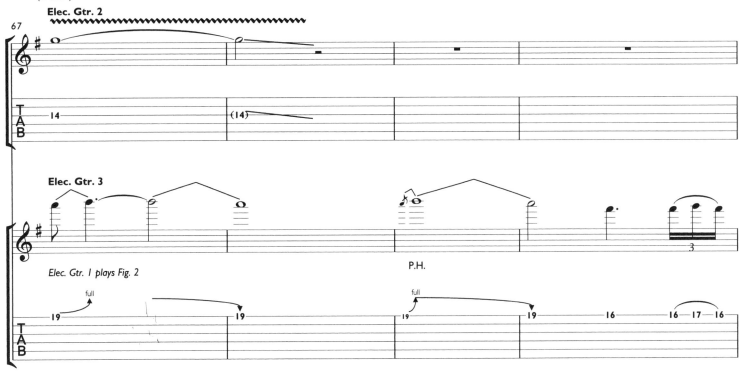

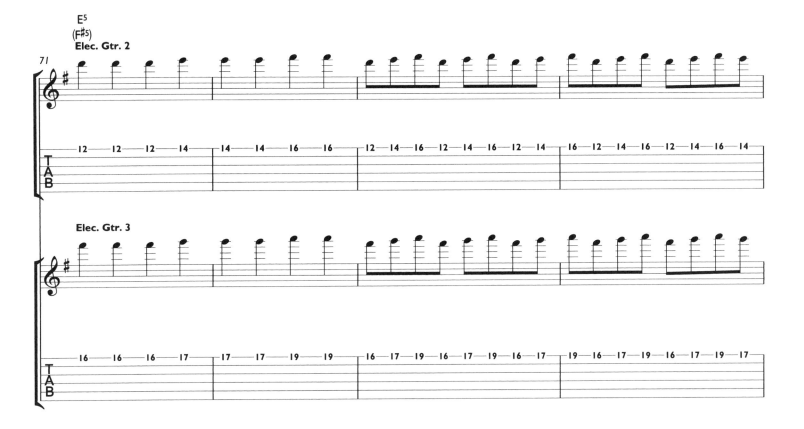

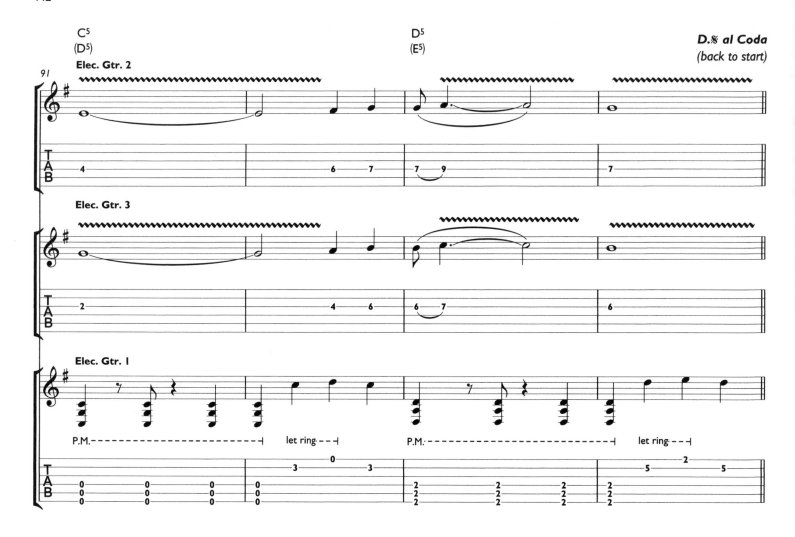

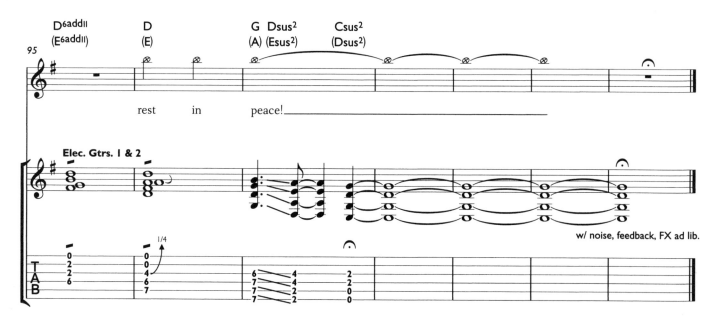

Notation and Tablature explained

Understanding chord boxes

Chord boxes show the neck of your guitar as if viewed head on—the vertical lines represent the strings (low E to high E, from left to right), and the horizontal lines represent the frets.

An **X** above a string means 'don't play this string'.
An **O** above a string means 'play this open string'.
The black dots show you where to put your fingers.

A curved line joining two dots on the fretboard represents a 'barre'. This means that you flatten one of your fingers (usually the first) so that you hold down all the strings between the two dots at the fret marked.

A fret marking at the side of the chord box shows you where chords that are played higher up the neck are located.

Tuning your guitar

The best way to tune your guitar is to use an electronic tuner. Alternatively, you can use relative tuning; this will ensure that your guitar is in tune with itself, but won't guarantee that you will be in tune with the original track (or any other musicians).

How to use relative tuning

Fret the low E string at the 5th fret and pluck; compare this with the sound of the open A string. The two notes should be in tune. If not, adjust the tuning of the A string until the two notes match.

Repeat this process for the other strings according to this diagram:

Note that the B string should match the note at the 4th fret of the G string, whereas all the other strings match the note at the 5th fret of the string below.

As a final check, ensure that the bottom E string and top E string are in tune with each other.

Detuning and Capo use

If the song uses an unconventional tuning, it will say so clearly at the top of the music, e.g. '6 = D' (tune string 6 to D) or 'detune guitar down by a semitone'. If a capo is used, it will tell you the fret number to which it must be attached. The standard notation will always be in the key at which the song sounds, but the guitar tab will take tuning changes into account. Just detune/add the capo and follow the fret numbers. The chord symbols will show the sounding chord above and the chord you actually play below in brackets.

Use of figures

In order to make the layout of scores clearer, figures that occur several times in a song will be numbered, e.g. 'Fig. 1', 'Fig. 2', etc. A dotted line underneath shows the extent of the 'figure'. When a phrase is to be played, it will be marked clearly in the score, along with the instrument that should play it.

Reading Guitar Tab

Guitar tablature illustrates the six strings of the guitar graphically, showing you where you put your fingers for each note or chord. It is always shown with a stave in standard musical notation above it. The guitar tablature stave has six lines, each of them representing a different string. The top line is the high E string, the second line being the B string, and so on. Instead of using note heads, guitar tab uses numbers which show the fret number to be stopped by the left hand. The rhythm is indicated underneath the tab stave. Ex. 1 (below) shows four examples of single notes.

Ex. 2 shows four different chords. The 3rd one (Asus4) should be played as a barre chord at the 5th fret. The 4th chord (C9) is a half, or jazz chord shape. You have to mute the string marked with an 'x' (the A string in this case) with a finger of your fretting hand in order to obtain the correct voicing.

Ex.1

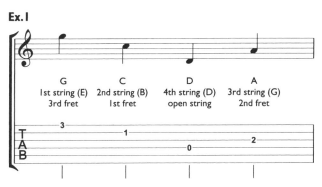

Ex.2

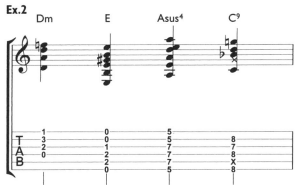

Notation of other guitar techniques

Picking hand techniques:

1. Down and up strokes

These symbols show that the first and third notes are to be played with a down stroke of the pick and the others up strokes.

2. Palm mute

Mute the notes with the palm of the picking hand by lightly touching the strings near the bridge.

3. Pick rake

Drag the pick across the indicated strings with a single sweep. The extra pressure will often mute the notes slightly and accentuate the final note.

4. Arpeggiated chords

Strum across the indicated strings in the direction of the arrow head of the wavy line.

5. Tremolo picking

Shown by the slashes on the stem of the note. Very fast alternate picking. Rapidly and continuously move the pick up and down on each note.

6. Pick scrape

Drag the edge of the pick up or down the lower strings to create a scraping sound.

7. Right hand tapping

'Tap' onto the note indicated by a '+' with a finger of the picking hand. It is nearly always followed by a pull-off to sound the note fretted below.

8. Tap slide

As with tapping, but the tapped note is slid randomly up the fretboard, then pulled off to the following note.

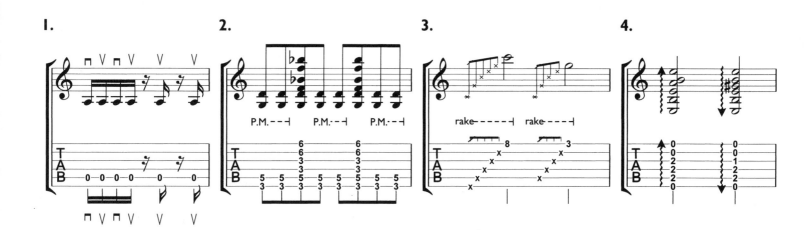

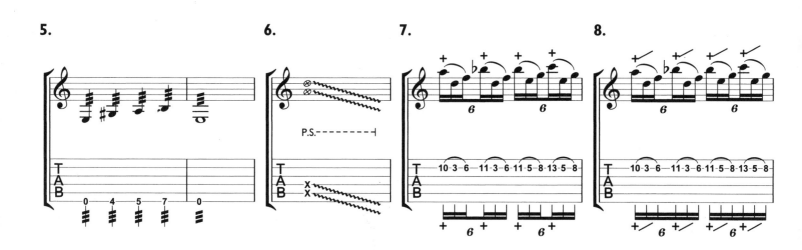